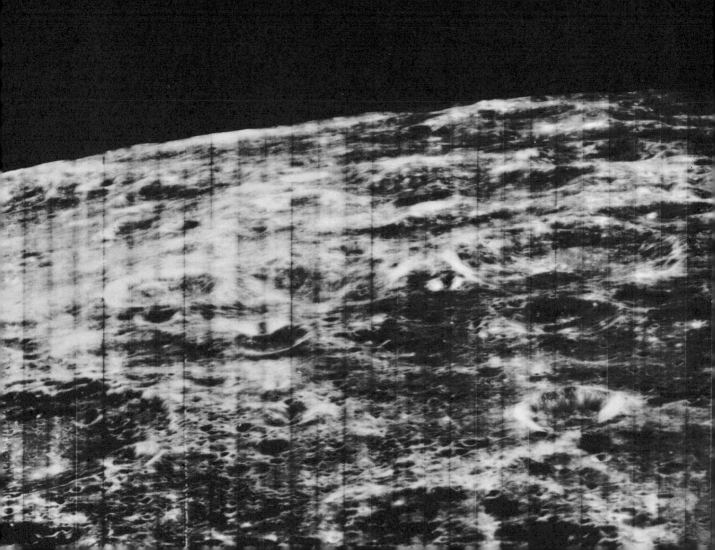

The Look-It-Up Book of
STARS AND PLANETS

PATRICIA LAUBER, formerly editor-in-chief of a young people's science magazine and Chief Editor, Science and Mathematics, for a leading children's encyclopedia, is the author of many books for children. She has written three LOOK-IT-UP Books and has contributed several titles to two other Random House series, Allabout Books and Gateway books. A graduate of Wellesley College, she now lives in New York City.

JOHN POLGREEN is a member of the Association of Lunar and Planetary Observers and of the American Association of Variable Star Observers. He has illustrated many books about astronomy and space, and wrote and illustrated THE EARTH IN SPACE in collaboration with his wife Cathleen, who is also an enthusiastic amateur astronomer. The Polgreens live in Dobbs Ferry, New York.

The Look-It-Up Book of
STARS AND PLANETS

by Patricia Lauber
Illustrated by John Polgreen

Random House · New York

We would like to thank
James S. Pickering, Astronomer Emeritus
of The American Museum of Natural History Hayden Planetarium,
for his thorough reading of the manuscript
and his most helpful comments.

Lick Observatory, University of California, Mount Hamilton, California, 33, 57, 58-59, 100 (bottom), 106, 122; Lowell Observatory, Flagstaff, Arizona, 120-121; Metropolitan Museum of Art, 4; Mount Wilson and Palomar Observatories, Carnegie Institution of Washington, California Institute of Technology, 7, 31, 32, 45, 61, 64, 65, 75, 78, 100 (top), 102, 109, 116, 125; National Aeronautic and Space Administration, endpapers, 25, 47, 60, 66; National Radio Astronomy Observatory, Green Bank, West Virginia, 5, 80, 81; New Mexico State University Observatory, 51; John Polgreen, 74, 95; Yerkes Observatory, University of Chicago, Williams Bay, Wisconsin, 2, 10-11, 27, 53.

Library of Congress Catalog Card Number: 67-21915

Manufactured in the United States of America

Printed by Copifier Lithograph Corp., Cleveland, Ohio

Designed by Janet Townsend

Stars and Planets

We are flying through space. Our craft is the earth, which orbits the sun at a speed of 67,000 miles an hour. As it orbits the sun, it spins on its axis.

The sun is a star. To us it seems much bigger and brighter than any star. But that is because we are very close to it. As stars go, the sun is neither very big nor very bright.

The sun is one star in a vast "island" of stars called a galaxy. There are billions of stars in our galaxy. And our galaxy is one of millions of galaxies in the universe.

None of these facts comes as a surprise today. Almost everyone knows that the universe is huge beyond imagining. Almost everyone knows that the earth is a small planet that travels around the star we call our sun.

Yet that is not what our eyes tell us. We do not see the universe spread out. The sun does not look like a star. We do not see the earth moving. We do not feel it rushing through space. Instead, the earth seems to be standing still while all things move around it.

For a very long time men believed what their eyes told them. Through most of human history, people have thought that the earth was the center of the universe. Then, bit by bit, the truth was discovered. It was discovered by astronomers, scientists who study the heavens. And it was one of the world's truly great discoveries.

Astronomers have made many other discoveries. They have found billions of stars that the eye alone cannot see. They have learned what stars are made of and why they shine. Astronomers have learned about other planets and moons in our solar system. They have found ways to measure the temperatures of stars and planets; to measure huge distances; to map the galaxy of which we are part.

In this book you will find many of the things that astronomers have discovered. And you will find the questions that they hope to answer as rockets carry men and instruments into space.

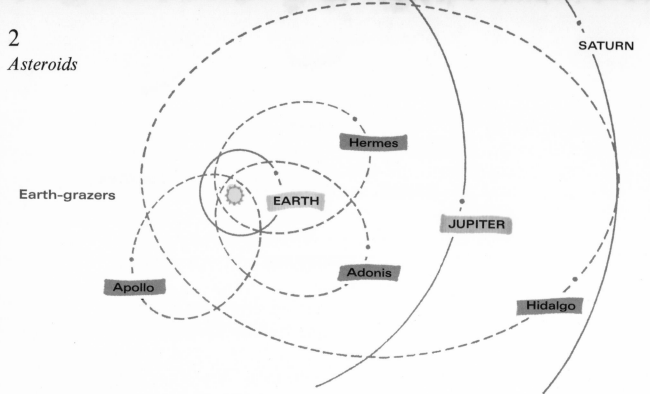

Earth-grazers

SATURN

Hermes

EARTH

JUPITER

Apollo

Adonis

Hidalgo

Asteroids About 200 years ago a German astronomer made a strange discovery. He found what seemed to be a gap in the solar system. There was, he thought, too much space between the orbits of Mars and Jupiter. He began to wonder about this space. Could there be an unknown planet in it? Was there a planet that astronomers had not discovered?

Other astronomers began to search the space. Their search led to the discovery of thousands of tiny planets.

The first discovery was made in 1801 by an Italian astronomer. He found what seemed to be an unknown star. At least, the tiny point of light was not listed in his star catalogs. He watched the light night after night. And he saw that it moved among the stars. He knew then that it could not be a star. Instead, it seemed to be a small object that was orbiting the sun. He named it Ceres.

Two asteroid trails among the stars

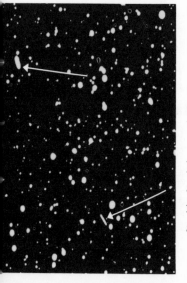

Ceres was very small. So astronomers went on searching for an unknown planet.

The next year a German astronomer discovered another small object in the gap. He named it Pallas. It was even smaller than Ceres. Soon two more of these objects were found—Juno and Vesta. Then still others were discovered.

Astronomers were not sure what the objects were. They moved like planets but looked like stars. The objects were given the name asteroids, which means "starlike bodies." (It is not a very good name, since the objects are really tiny planets. That is why they are sometimes called planetoids, which means "planetlike bodies.")

Since then thousands of asteroids have been found. Of these, 1,600 have been named. At first the asteroids were named after

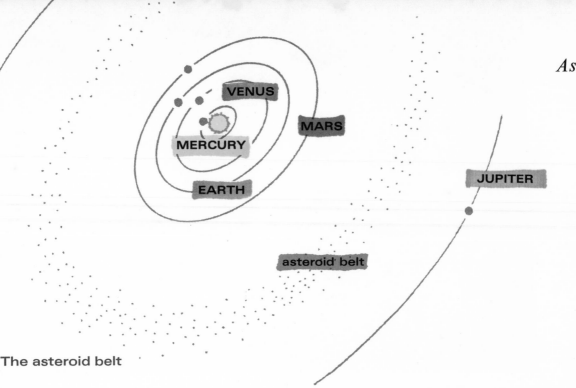

The asteroid belt

gods and goddesses of ancient Greece and Rome. But astronomers soon ran out of such names. They began to name asteroids after their wives, children, and pets. That is why some have names like Jenny, Margo, Tynka, Mimi, and Santa.

Most of the asteroids stay between the orbits of Mars and Jupiter. Some take $1\frac{1}{2}$ years to orbit the sun. Others take 6 years.

A few asteroids do not stay within that belt of space. One of these is Hermes. Hermes sometimes passes very close to the earth's orbit. It once came within 485,000 miles of the earth. It is one of the asteroids known as Earth-grazers. Apollo and Adonis are two other Earth-grazers. Hidalgo also leaves the belt. It swings out as far as the orbit of Saturn. Several asteroids travel in Jupiter's orbit.

A few asteroids leave space. They become meteorites. If you have ever touched a meteorite, you may have touched an asteroid.

All the asteroids are very small. Ceres is the largest. It is about 500 miles wide. The smallest known asteroids are the size of large rocks. Because they are small, asteroids are hard to see and study. Not very much is known about them.

At one time scientists thought the asteroids might be pieces of a shattered planet. Today many astronomers have a different idea. They think the asteroids are part of a planet that never formed. At a time when the other planets were taking shape, this one failed to form. Its material became the asteroids.

But no one is sure what happened. The asteroids are one of the mysteries in astronomy.

Astrology   *See* ASTRONOMY

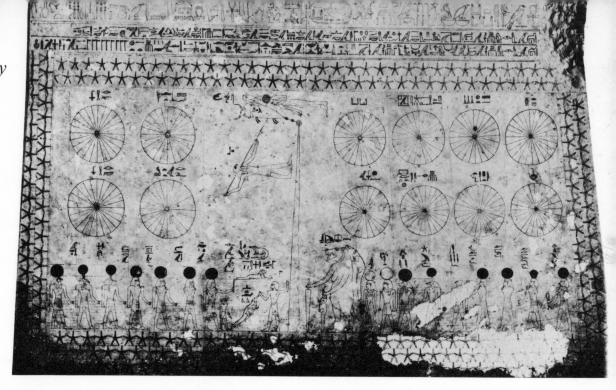

Ancient Egyptian priests used this chart to keep track of the stars.

Astronomy   Astronomy is the study of the heavens. It is the science of the universe, of everything in space. Astronomers study the sun, the planets and their moons, meteors, comets, and stars. They study the galaxies, which are huge "islands" of stars.

Astronomy is the oldest of the sciences. Its roots go back thousands of years. Long before people learned to read and write, they learned to study the heavens.

As the sun sets and the sky darkens, the stars come out. The black sky sparkles with countless twinkling lights. Early peoples looked with wonder at this night sky. In time they began to know the stars. They learned that the stars formed patterns in the sky. Some patterns appeared with the coming of spring, summer, autumn, or winter. Some stars could always be seen, no matter what the season. People began to use the stars. They used stars as guides. They used star patterns to keep track of the seasons.

Later, people began to settle in villages. Villages became towns. Still later, the first great civilizations arose. Then, the study of the heavens became very important. The high priests studied the movements of the sun, the moon, the planets, and the stars. They believed that they could read the future in these movements and that heavenly bodies controlled men's lives. This belief became the so-called science of astrology. The belief was wrong. But it led to the first careful studies of the heavens. From these studies came the true science of astronomy.

Today astronomers still study the heavens. But they do so in ways that ancient astronomers never even dreamed of. With mod-

Modern astronomers use instruments like this radio telescope.

ern instruments they study what the human eye alone cannot see. They study things that are trillions of miles away. They discover what stars are made of. They have found distant galaxies made up of billions of stars.

Close at hand are the moon, Mars, and Venus. Astronomers have long dreamed of visiting the moon and planets. Modern rockets are making this dream come true. As explorers go into space, astronomy leaps forward. The oldest science is also one of the most modern sciences.

Atmosphere The earth is wrapped in a blanket of gases. These gases form the earth's atmosphere, which we also call "the air."

There are about 20 different gases in our atmosphere. The two main ones are nitrogen and oxygen. The air is nearly four fifths nitrogen and one fifth oxygen. Oxygen is the gas that almost all forms of life must have. Another gas in the air is carbon dioxide. Green plants use this gas when they are making their food. There are traces of other gases. Some of these are helium, hydrogen, argon, krypton, neon, xenon, and ozone; ozone is a special form of oxygen.

Many other heavenly bodies also have atmospheres. The stars do. So do the other planets in our solar system. But none of the planets has an atmosphere like the earth's. Mercury, for example, has just a trace of an atmosphere. Jupiter has a huge atmosphere. Two of the main gases in it are methane and ammonia. Both are poisonous to us.

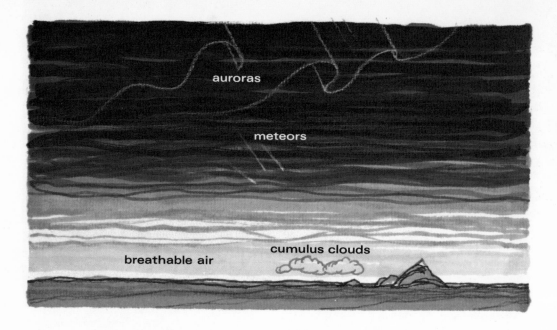

Our atmosphere is one of the things that make the earth a planet of life. It is the air we breathe. It blocks certain dangerous rays sent out by the sun. It keeps the earth from getting very hot or very cold.

Atoms A table, a star, and a planet are all made of matter. You are made of matter. So are the oceans, the air, and the moon. Matter can be a solid, a liquid, or a gas. It is anything that takes up space and has weight.

All matter can be broken up into tiny pieces called molecules. A molecule is the smallest piece that is still like the original matter. For example, a water molecule is still like water.

A molecule can be broken into even smaller parts. These are called atoms. A water molecule, for example, can be broken into three atoms—two atoms of hydrogen and one atom of oxygen.

Atoms are sometimes called the building blocks of matter. All the kinds of matter in the world are made from atoms. You might say that atoms are like the letters of the alphabet. There are only 26 letters in our alphabet. But those 26 letters can be put together in many, many ways. They can be used to make hundreds of thousands of words.

More than 100 kinds of atoms are known. Some have been created in laboratories. The others exist in nature. But most exist only in very small quantities. Most kinds of matter are made from about 20 kinds of atoms.

Sometimes atoms of one kind are joined together. They form molecules of the chemical elements. Hydrogen, helium, and oxygen are three elements.

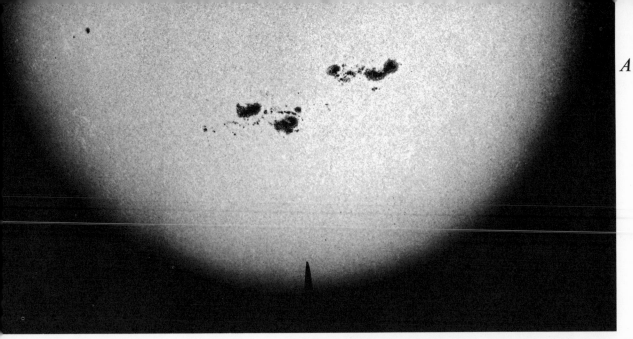

Auroras often appear after sunspots develop.

Sometimes atoms of different kinds are joined together. They form molecules of chemical compounds. Water is a chemical compound. It is made of two elements—oxygen and hydrogen.

Atoms are tiny. They are so small that they cannot be seen with even the most powerful microscope. They are so small that 25 million atoms could be lined up across the head of a pin.

Yet atoms themselves are made up of even smaller pieces. These pieces are called atomic particles.

There are three main kinds of atomic particle: protons, neutrons, and electrons. The protons and neutrons are bunched together in the middle of an atom. The bunch is called the nucleus. (The plural of "nucleus" is "nuclei.") The electrons orbit the nucleus.

Auroras Sometimes the night sky is filled with shifting, glowing lights. The lights may arch across the sky. Or they may look like a curtain. Streamers and rays of light reach upward from the arch or curtain. The lights may last for hours.

These lights are called auroras. Those of the Northern Hemisphere are called aurora borealis, or northern lights. Those of the South-

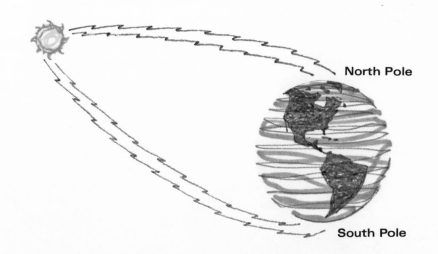

North Pole

South Pole

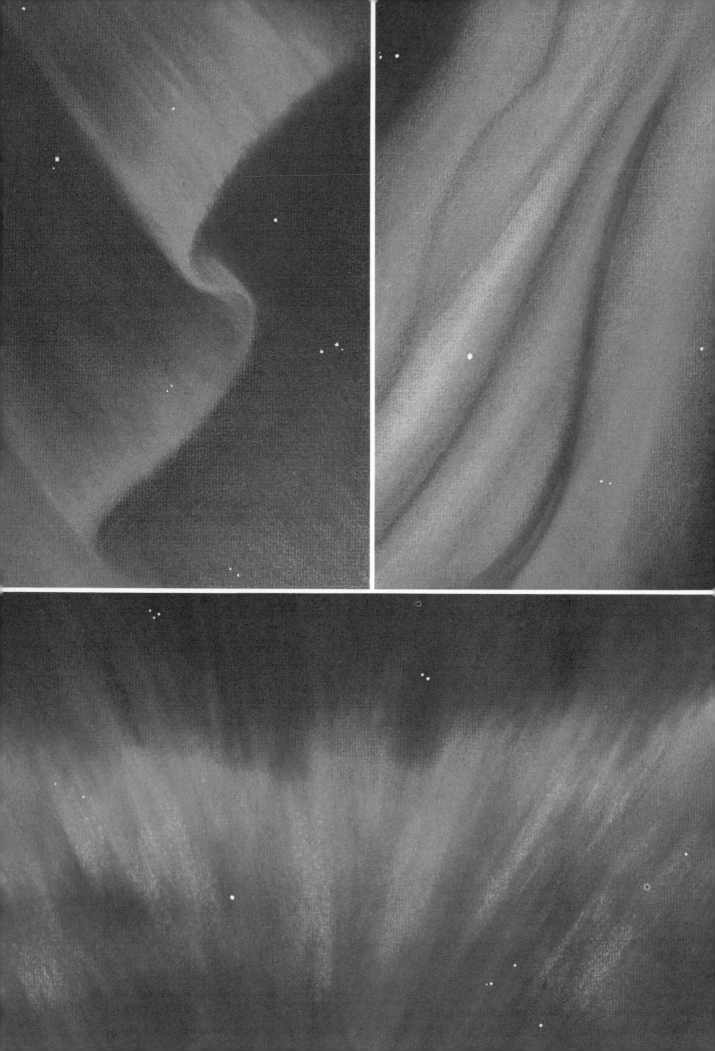

The shifting, glowing lights
that sometimes fill the night sky
are called auroras.

ern Hemisphere are called aurora australis, or southern lights. Auroras are most often seen in the polar regions. They are almost never seen near the equator. In the United States they are seldom seen south of San Francisco and Atlanta.

Auroras are caused by an electrical charge in the upper atmosphere. It makes the air glow. The electric charge comes from the sun. Sometimes the sun sends out huge bursts of gas particles that carry an electric charge. When the particles strike the atmosphere near the poles, auroras appear. They appear at the same time in both hemispheres. They are most likely to appear a few days after a large group of sunspots develops on the sun.
See also: SUN

Axis Suppose you take a steel knitting needle and an orange. You push the needle through the center of the orange, from bottom to top. You then spin the orange on the needle. The orange is spinning on its axis.

An axis is a straight line around which a body spins. The line can be real, like the needle. Or it can be imaginary. The earth's axis is an imaginary line that runs through the center of the earth. One point where it comes out is the North Pole. The other is the South Pole.

Every rotating, or spinning, body has an axis. The planets and their moons do. So does the sun and every star.

The plural of "axis" is "axes."

Binary Stars *See* STARS

Celestial Equator *See* SEASONS
Celestial Poles *See* SEASONS
Celestial Sphere *See* SEASONS

Comets Sometimes—but not very often—it is possible to see a comet in the night sky. The comet appears as a bright, ball-shaped head of light with a long, glowing tail. Comets move very fast. But they are so far away that they appear to move slowly. To see a comet move you must watch it over several weeks.

Comets are members of the solar system. That is, they are captives of the sun. They travel around it in huge, sausage-shaped orbits. Comets cannot be seen when they are far from the sun. They shine only when they are near the sun.

Comets seem to be made chiefly of frozen gases and dust. Astronomers say that a distant comet is like a huge, dirty snowball. The snowball is probably about half a mile wide. As a comet nears the sun, it is warmed. The frozen gases change from ice to vapor. The sun's rays pass through the gases and cause them to glow. A head of glowing gases forms around the snowball core.

The gases are very light. They are so light that the sun's rays push them away from the sun. That is how a comet's tail forms. The tail always points away from the sun. When a comet is nearing the sun, the tail streams behind or to one side. When a comet is moving away from the sun, the tail goes first.

By that time the comet is very large. The head may measure a million miles across and the tail may stretch through millions of miles of space. The comet moves on, leaving the sun behind. The tail shrinks and vanishes. The head also shrinks. It stops glowing. The comet again becomes a huge, dirty snowball.

The orbit of Halley's Comet.

NEPTUNE

Halley's Comet

URANUS

SATURN

JUPITER

MARS

EARTH

The orbits of comets are of different sizes. Some comets take 3 years to make one orbit. Some take 6 years. Some take 100 years. Others may take thousands of years.

About a dozen comets approach the sun each year. Most can be seen only through a telescope. Only a few are big enough and bright enough to be seen easily. One of these is Halley's comet. It orbits the sun once every 75 to 77 years. It was last seen in 1910. It should appear again in 1985 or 1986.

A few comets are discovered every year. They may be newly formed comets. Or they may be older comets that no one saw before. Astronomers cannot tell. They do not know whether new comets keep forming in space.

They do know that comets don't last forever. On each trip around the sun a comet loses some of its dust and gas. Finally all the gases vanish. Nothing is left except the dust. The dust is strewn along the path that the comet used to follow. The particles of dust go on orbiting the sun. Sometimes the earth passes through a swarm of these dust particles. They enter the atmosphere, and a meteor shower takes place.

Every August, for example, the earth crosses the path of a vanished comet. We then see a meteor shower. The shower looks as if it were coming from the constellation Perseus. So it is called the Perseid meteor shower. This shower takes place around August 12. If you watch the sky after midnight, you may see a meteor a minute.

The Greek alphabet. Our word "alphabet" comes from the names of the first two letters.

alpha beta gamma delta epsilon zeta eta theta

iota kappa lambda mu nu xi omicron pi

rho sigma tau upsilon phi chi psi omega

Constellations

The stars are far-flung in space. Trillions and trillions of miles separate a star from its nearest neighbors. But as seen from the earth, the stars appear to be in groups. A group forms a pattern in the sky. There is a name for these patterns, or groups—constellations. The name comes from a Latin word meaning "group of stars."

For thousands of years men have been picking out patterns in the night sky. They have found the shapes of things, animals, and people. They have given names to these shapes and made up stories about them. We still use some of these shapes and names today. Many of them have come to us from ancient Greece and Rome.

Constellations are a handy way of mapping the sky. And so it is useful to talk as if the stars really were in groups.

It is also useful to talk about the way they move across the sky. As you know, they only seem to do this. It is really the earth that is moving. The earth turns. And stars appear to rise and set at night. The earth journeys around the sun. And we see a parade of different constellations across the sky during the year. With each season different constellations come into view.

All told there are 88 constellations. Of these 48 are in the Northern Hemisphere. The other 40 are in the Southern Hemisphere. Every star that can be seen with the unaided eye belongs to one of these constellations.

Many of the brightest stars were long ago given names of their own. We still use some of these names. Mizar, Hamal, and Deneb are three stars that were named by Arab astronomers. Pollux, Castor, and Procyon are three that were named by the Greeks.

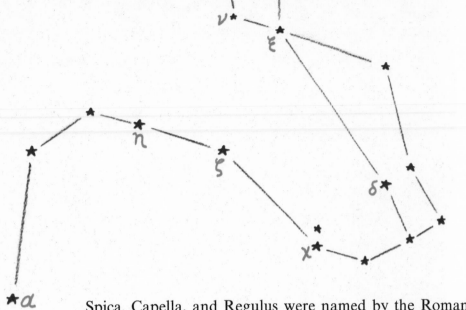

DRACO

Spica, Capella, and Regulus were named by the Romans.

Some stars are labeled with letters of the Greek alphabet. For example, Alpha [α] is the Greek *a,* and Beta [β] is the Greek *b.* Alpha [α] Draconis is therefore star *a* in the constellation of Draco. Beta [β] Draconis is star *b.* In other constellations the stars are numbered from west to east. 61 Cygni is the 61st star in Cygnus. Stars are also referred to by their catalog numbers.

STAR-GAZING

What stars can you see on a clear night? The answer depends on three things:

WHERE YOU LIVE. Suppose you move from Ontario to Florida. You will find some familiar constellations in Florida's sky. You will find other constellations that are new to you.

THE SEASON. Many constellations change with the seasons. You will see different constellations in different seasons.

THE HOUR. At night constellations move across the sky. The sky you see at 2 a.m. will be different from the one you saw at 9 p.m.

The best way to learn the stars is to get a star map for the region where you live. You will find instructions on the map. They will tell you how to use it at different seasons and hours.

Meanwhile, you can use the maps on the next few pages. They may not be quite right for your region. But you can probably use them anyway. They show constellations seen by people who live at about 40 degrees north latitude. This takes in a belt running across the United States from New York to San Francisco. The maps show the constellations as they appear around 9 p.m.

Can you find the Little Dipper ?

POLAR CONSTELLATIONS

Certain constellations can be seen all year round. These are the north polar constellations. They move in the sky as the year passes. But they can always be seen. They are good constellations to learn first. You can use them to find many other constellations.

To use the map, go outdoors about 9 o'clock on a clear evening. Face north. East is then to your right and west to your left. Hold the book open in front of you. Hold it so that the current month is at the top. Use a weak flashlight to read the map. (This is easiest if you have a friend to hold the light or the book.)

Start by finding Ursa Major, the Great Bear. This constellation contains the stars known as the Big Dipper.

Find the two stars at the end of the Big Dipper's bowl. Imagine a line drawn through the two stars and reaching beyond them. This line will lead you to Polaris, the North Star.

Once you have found Polaris, you have found the Little Dipper. Polaris is the end star in the handle of the Little Dipper. (The Little Dipper is also called Ursa Minor, the Little Bear.)

Make the line go on past Polaris. It will bring you to Cassiopeia, the Queen. The five main stars in Cassiopeia form a wide W or M.

THE NORTH POLAR CONSTELLATIONS

See if you can find Draco and Cepheus. (Draco is easiest to see in late spring and early summer.)

People who live in the Southern Hemisphere see the south polar constellations. The best known of these is Crux Australis, the Southern Cross.

Can you find Leo?

SEASONAL CONSTELLATIONS

The next star maps are for the seasons. They show the sky as it appears in early April, July, October, and January. To use one of the maps, go outdoors about 9 p.m. Face south with east to your right and west to your left. Hold the book open in front of you.

SPRING STARS

Leo, the Lion, is a sign of spring. When you see Leo appear in the east, spring is on the way. The stars of Leo's head form a sickle. Find the sickle by imagining a line through the two stars at the back of the Big Dipper's bowl. Follow the line south and you come to the sickle. Now imagine a line through the two front stars of the bowl. It leads you to the triangle that is the back part of Leo. Leo is also easy to find because of the very bright star that forms his heart. The star is named Regulus. In the triangle there is a slightly less bright star. This is Denebola.

Gemini, the Twins, are winter stars that can still be seen in spring. Look for them in the western sky. The constellation has two bright stars, Castor and Pollux. They are very close together.

Follow the curve in the handle of the Big Dipper. It brings you to Boötes, the Herdsman. In Boötes is the very bright, orange star named Arcturus.

Follow the same curve through Arcturus. You will come to another very bright star. It is called Spica. Spica is in the constellation Virgo, the Virgin.

South of Virgo and Leo you will find Hydra, the Serpent. This winding constellation is the longest in the sky.

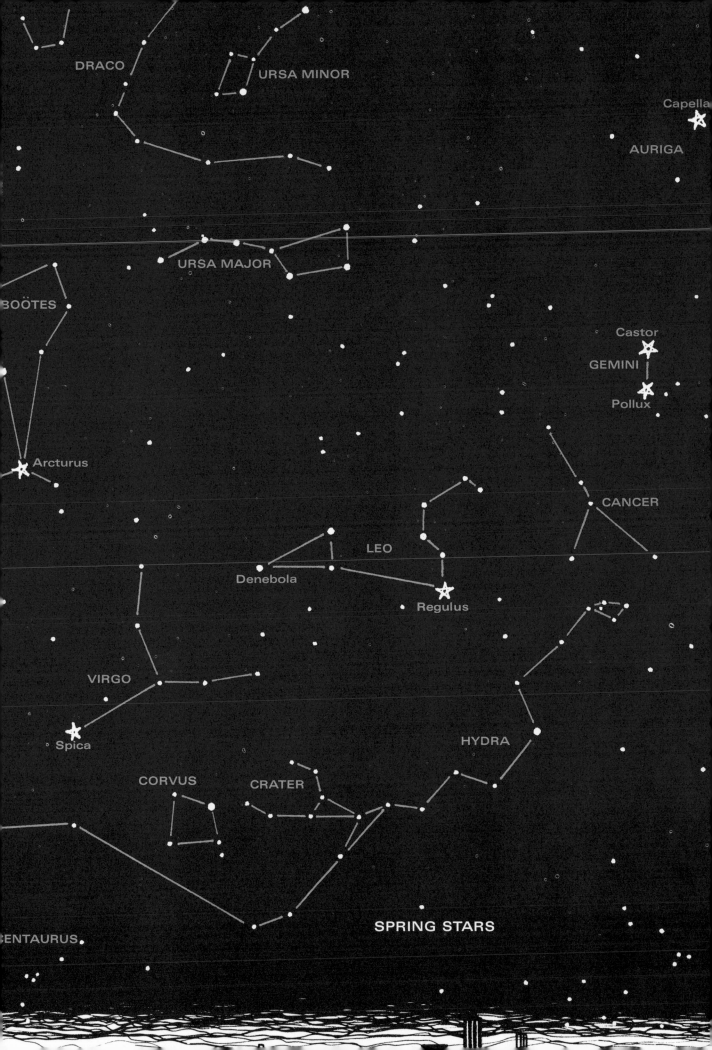

Can you find Boötes?

SUMMER STARS

Summer is the best time to observe the Milky Way. The Milky Way is then a sparkling cloud that stretches across the sky. The summer sky also has many constellations and about six very bright stars.

Boötes, with its bright star Arcturus, can still be seen.

East of Boötes you can see Corona Borealis, the Northern Crown. It is a half circle of stars.

South and east of Boötes is Scorpius, the Scorpion. Its stars form a fishhook in the sky, and they are easy to find. One of them is the bright and red star Antares.

East of the Crown is Hercules, a sprawling constellation. At its center is an uneven square formed by four stars.

East of Hercules is a triangle of three very bright stars. (In late summer they are nearly overhead.) Each belongs to a different constellation. Deneb is in Cygnus, the Swan. Vega is in Lyra, the Lyre. Altair is in Aquila, the Eagle. Vega is the second brightest star in the summer sky. Only Arcturus is brighter.

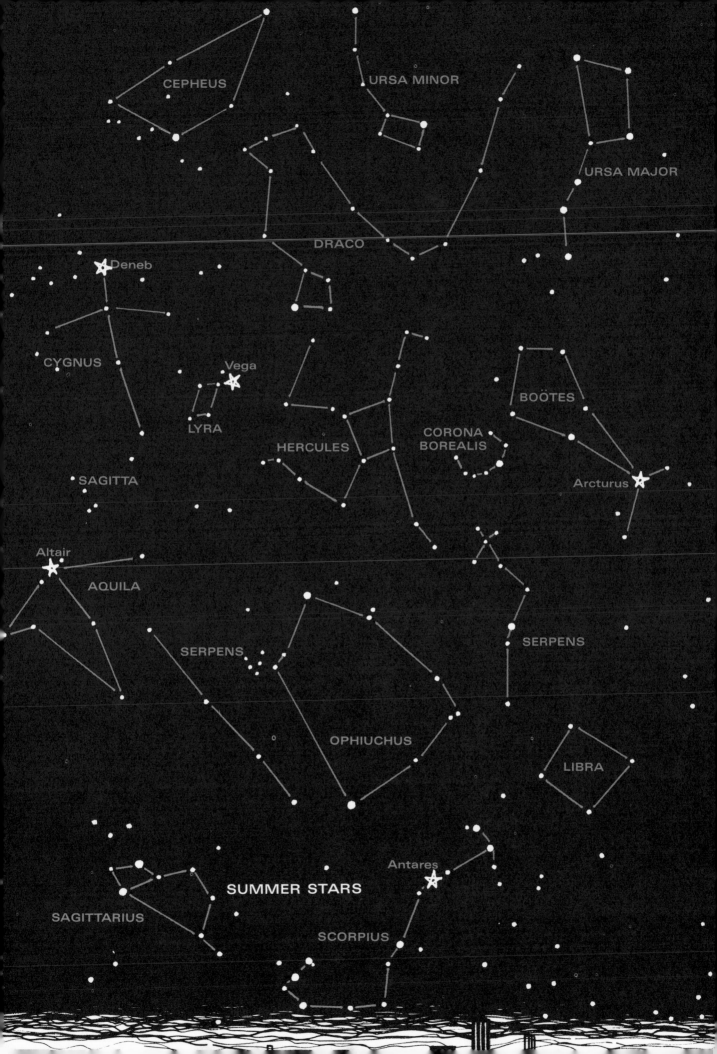

CEPHEUS

URSA MINOR

URSA MAJOR

DRACO

Deneb

CYGNUS

Vega

BOÖTES

LYRA

HERCULES

CORONA
BOREALIS

SAGITTA

Arcturus

Altair

AQUILA

SERPENS

SERPENS

OPHIUCHUS

LIBRA

Antares

SUMMER STARS

SAGITTARIUS

SCORPIUS

Can you find Pegasus?

AUTUMN STARS

In autumn a number of summer constellations can still be seen—Lyra, Cygnus, and Aquila are clear in the west. The new constellations are not very bright. The best known is Pegasus, the Winged Horse. The main part of Pegasus is a huge, uneven square. Its four corners are marked by bright stars. To find the square, imagine a line from Polaris through the west end of Cassiopeia. This line leads you to the eastern side of the square.

East of Pegasus are two long lines of stars—the constellation Andromeda. In Andromeda you can see a fuzzy patch. This is the Andromeda Galaxy, often called M 31. It looks as if it were part of Andromeda. But it is really a vast "island" of stars that lies far, far beyond the stars of Andromeda.

South of Andromeda is Cetus, the Whale. The most interesting star in Cetus is Mira. Mira is a variable star. That is, its brightness varies. Sometimes Mira is so dim that it cannot be seen without a telescope. In about 120 days Mira brightens. It can easily be seen with the unaided eye. Then it dims again.

There is only one really bright star in the autumn sky. This is Fomalhaut. It is in Piscis Austrinus, the Southern Fish. To find the star, go back to the square in Pegasus. Imagine a line through the two western stars in the square. Follow it south. It should lead you to Fomalhaut, near the southern horizon.

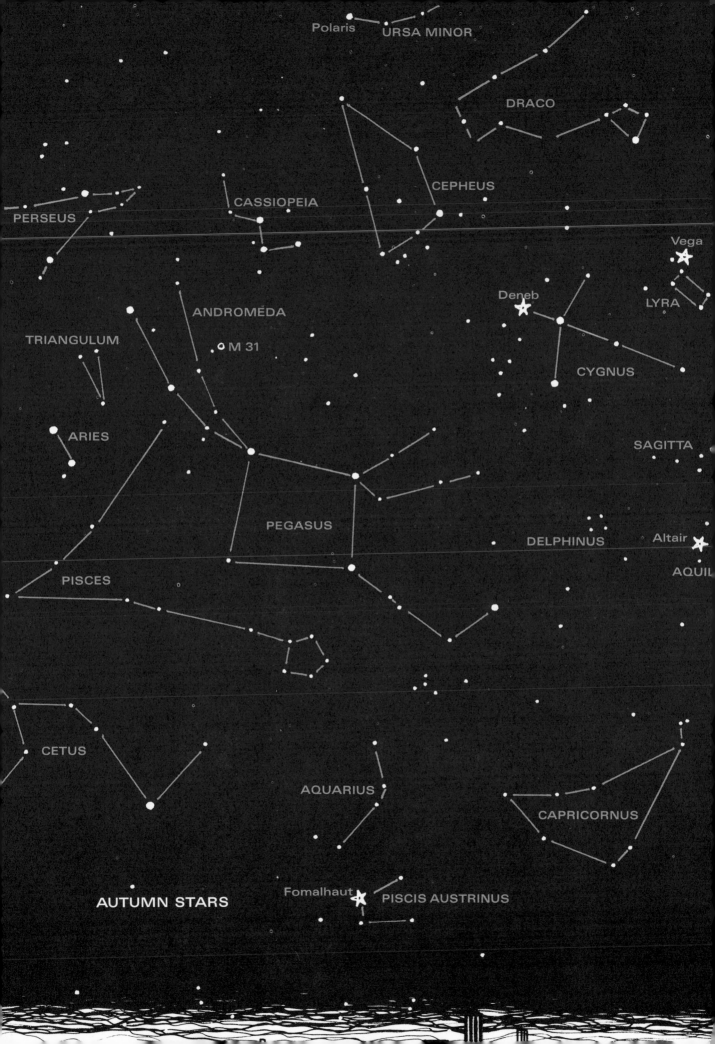

Can you find Orion?

WINTER STARS

In the clear skies of winter, Orion, the Hunter, is easy to find. Orion has more bright stars than any other constellation.

Orion's body is four-sided. Four bright stars mark its corners. Two of them are very bright. Betelgeuse is one of these. It is a red supergiant and a variable star. Rigel is the other. It is a blue-white supergiant. It is also a double star. Within the rectangle are the three bright stars of Orion's belt. Hanging from the belt is a faint sword. The easiest way to find Orion is to look for the belt.

Orion can be seen from most parts of Canada and the United States.

Use the stars in Orion's belt as a pointer. Follow the pointer to the southeast and you find Sirius, the Dog Star. Sirius is the brightest star in the sky. It is part of the constellation Canis Major, the Big Dog.

Go back to Betelgeuse in Orion. Imagine a line reaching eastward. It brings you to Canis Minor, the Little Dog. The unaided eye sees only two of the stars in Canis Minor. One of them is the very bright star Procyon. Procyon, Betelgeuse, and Sirius form a triangle in the sky.

Again use the stars in Orion's belt as a pointer. This time follow them to the northwest. You will find the constellation Taurus, the Bull. The Bull's head is a V-shaped group of stars. One of them is the red and very bright star Aldebaran. It is a double star.

At the Bull's shoulder are the Pleiades. They are an open cluster of several hundred stars. Six or seven of these stars can be seen with the unaided eye.

North of Taurus is the constellation Auriga, the Charioteer. Auriga is a five-sided figure. One of its stars is the brilliant, yellow Capella.

East of Auriga is Gemini, which can still be seen in spring.
See also: STARS; ZODIAC

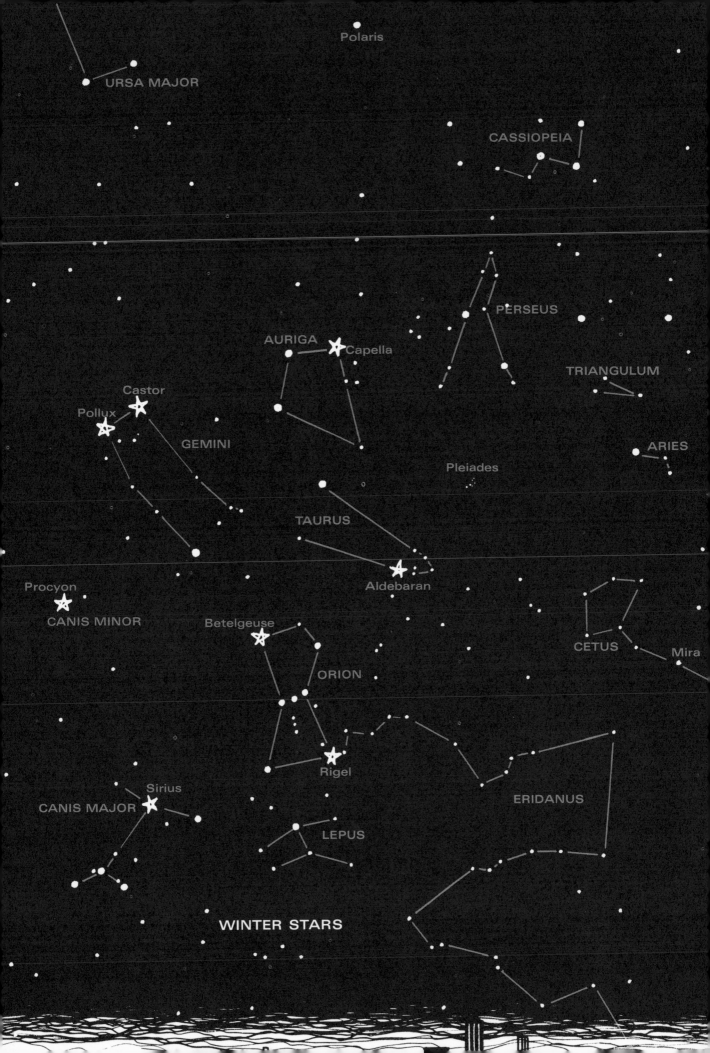

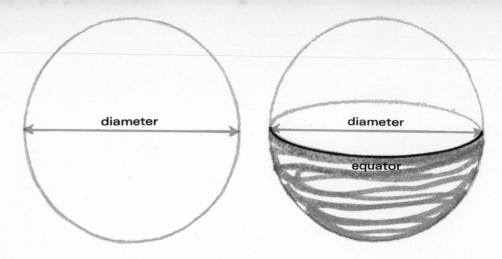

Cosmic Rays   Cosmic rays are atomic particles—parts of atoms. They have great energy, and they travel at nearly the speed of light (about 186,000 miles a second). The cosmic rays that reach the earth seem to come mostly from the sun. Some may come from the stars and from the remains of stars that have exploded. They may also come from outside our own galaxy.

The cosmic rays from space are called primary cosmic rays. They are dangerous to life. Fortunately, they do not reach the surface of the earth. Instead, they are trapped by the earth's magnetic field.

The primary rays, however, do strike the earth's atmosphere. They break up some of its atoms. The splintered atoms give off rays that shower down on the earth. Particles from the broken-up atoms also shower down on the earth. Together the rays and particles are called secondary cosmic rays.

Secondary cosmic rays have great energy. They enter and pass through almost all forms of matter. They can pass through 3 feet of lead or 3,000 feet of water. They also pass through us, even though we don't feel them. The secondary rays are not harmful.

Day   *See* TIME

Diameter   Take a compass and draw a circle. Then take a ruler and draw a straight line across the circle. The line must pass through the center of the circle. It must end where it touches the circle at two points. The line you have drawn is the diameter of the circle.

Now suppose you have a globe, or sphere. Its diameter is a straight line that passes through the center. It reaches from one side of the globe to the far side. That is what is meant by the diameter of a planet, moon, or other sphere. Such a diameter is usually measured from pole to pole or at the equator.

Doppler Effect   *See* SPECTRUM
Dwarf Stars   *See* STARS

Earth from a manned spacecraft. The long tongue of land on the right is Florida.

Earth The earth is our home planet. This fact makes the earth very special. It is a planet of life. More important, it is a planet of intelligent life. It is the only such planet in our solar system.

The earth is one of a family of 9 planets. All of them orbit the star we call the sun. The earth is the third planet out from the sun. A fairly small planet, it is a ball of rock and metal. Wrapped around it is a thin blanket of air. Much of the earth's surface is covered with water.

There are many things about this small planet that make it just right for life.

One is the earth's distance from the sun. The earth is about 93 million miles from the sun. That is a good distance. The earth receives plenty of light and heat. But it does not broil in the sun's rays.

The shape of the earth's orbit is also good. The orbit is very nearly a circle. The earth is always about the same distance from the sun. It receives a steady supply of light and heat.

As the earth orbits the sun, you notice certain changes. The lengths of days change. So do the temperatures. That is, the earth has seasons. The seasons exist because of the way the earth's axis is tilted. Each pole is tilted toward the sun for part of the year. It is tilted away from the sun for part of the year.

Summer comes to the Northern Hemisphere when the North Pole is tilted toward the sun. Winter comes when the North Pole is tilted away.

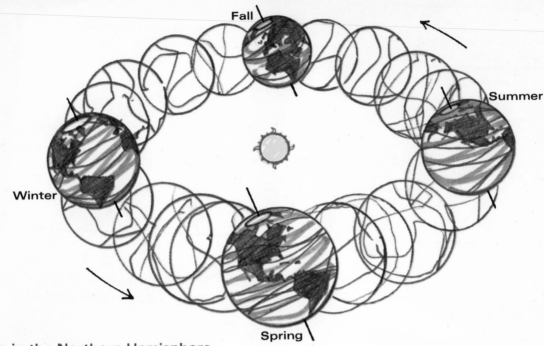

Seasons in the Northern Hemisphere.

The tilt of the axis makes our planet a very pleasant place. Every part of the earth gets some sunlight. Only the region at the equator is hot the year round. Only the polar regions ever get very cold. Most parts of the earth enjoy comfortable temperatures. They warm up or cool off as the seasons change.

While the earth is orbiting the sun, it is also spinning on its axis. During one orbit it spins about 365 times. As we see it, the sun appears to rise (and set) 365 times. When the earth makes one orbit, we say a year has passed. Each time it spins once, we say a day has passed.

During a day most parts of the earth pass from darkness into light and back into darkness. Only the polar regions ever have weeks of light and weeks of darkness. The rest of the earth has day and night. A place warms by day and cools off by night.

This warming and cooling is gentle. The earth does not become very hot by day and very cold by night. The temperature changes only a few degrees. For this we can thank the atmosphere—the envelope of air that surrounds the earth. It is another thing that makes the earth a planet of life.

By day the atmosphere acts as a shield. It lets through only some of the sun's light and heat. It filters out dangerous rays from the sun. By night the atmosphere acts as a blanket. It traps some of the day's heat and keeps it from escaping into space.

The atmosphere is made of gases. The two main gases in it are nitrogen and oxygen. There are traces of other gases in it, too—carbon dioxide, helium, hydrogen, and others. Without the at-

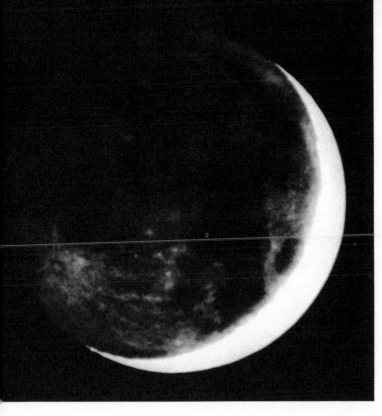

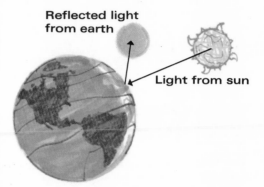

Reflected light
from earth

Light from sun

The bright crescent of the moon
is lighted by the sun. The rest
of the moon can be seen
because earthlight falls on it.

mosphere we could not live on the earth. It is the air we breathe.
Oxygen is the gas almost all forms of life need. Carbon dioxide is
the gas that green plants use when making their food.

The earth's gravity holds the atmosphere captive. If gravity
were weaker, most or all of the atmosphere would have escaped.

The strength of gravity depends on the size of a planet and the
material it is made of. The gravity of our small, rocky ball is just
right for life.

See also: MOON; SEASONS

THE EARTH	
average diameter	7,900 miles
average distance from sun	93,000,000 miles
average speed in orbit	67,000 miles an hour
time to make one orbit	$365\frac{1}{4}$ days
time to spin once	23 hours, 56 minutes
number of moons	1

Earthlight, *or* **Earthshine** The earth reflects the sun's light. Some of this light falls on the moon. It is called earthlight, or earthshine.

You can see earthlight. Look at the moon when it is in a crescent phase. You see the crescent—a bright, curved sliver. This part of the moon is lighted by the sun. You also see the rest of the moon, although it is much darker. You see this part of the moon because earthlight is falling on it.

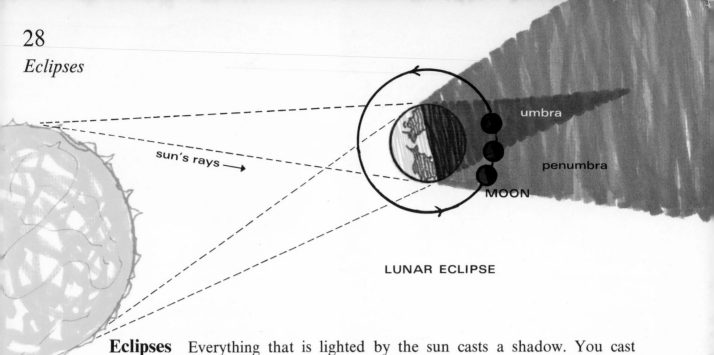

sun's rays →

umbra

penumbra

MOON

LUNAR ECLIPSE

Eclipses Everything that is lighted by the sun casts a shadow. You cast a shadow. So do houses, trees, and flagpoles. And so does the earth. One side of the earth is lighted by the sun. On the far side the earth casts its shadow in space. As the earth travels around the sun, so does its shadow.

Most of the time we do not see this shadow. But every now and then we do. As the moon orbits the earth, it sometimes passes into the shadow. We then see the earth's round shadow on the face of the full moon.

When that happens, the moon is no longer directly lighted by the sun. It is eclipsed, or dimmed. That is, a lunar eclipse is taking place. (*Lunar* means "of the moon.") When a lunar eclipse occurs, it can be seen from all over the night side of the earth.

The moon orbits the earth about once every 28 days. This means that it catches up with the earth's shadow about once a month. But it does not always pass through the shadow. The moon often passes above or below the shadow.

An eclipse takes place only when the moon passes through the shadow. Sometimes the whole moon passes through the shadow. This is called a total lunar eclipse. Sometimes only part of the moon passes through the shadow. This is called a partial eclipse.

You may find an eclipse called umbral or penumbral. These terms have to do with shadows. A shadow is darker at the center than toward the edges. At the center of the earth's shadow there is a circle of darkness. It is called the umbra from a Latin word for "shadow." Around it is a bigger, less dark circle. It is called the penumbra from Latin words meaning "almost a shadow."

The moon may pass through the umbra of the earth's shadow. Then an umbral eclipse takes place. Or it may pass through the penumbra. Then a penumbral eclipse takes place.

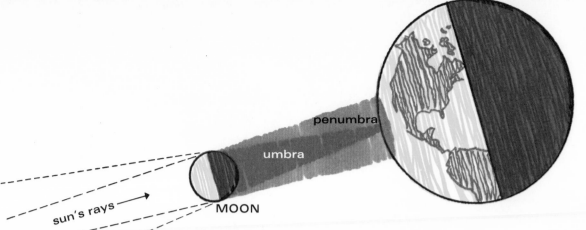

penumbra

umbra

sun's rays

MOON

SOLAR ECLIPSE

total eclipse

partial eclipse

annular eclipse

SOLAR ECLIPSES

Sometimes the moon's shadow falls on the earth. This can happen only when the moon is new—when it is between the sun and earth. If the sun, moon, and earth are lined up just so, the moon's shadow falls on the earth. A person within the shadow sees the moon hide the sun. This is a solar eclipse—an eclipse of the sun.

The shadow cast by the moon has an umbra and a penumbra.

The umbra is a dark circle 60 to 170 miles wide. It sweeps rapidly across the earth's face. If you are in the path of the umbra, you see a total eclipse. The moon moves across the sun's bright disk. The disk is hidden behind the moon for a few minutes. Then the moon moves on.

The penumbra falls on a much bigger area, for it is much bigger. It reaches out about 2,500 miles beyond the rim of the umbra. If you are in its path, you see a partial eclipse.

A total eclipse can take place only when the moon is fairly close to the earth. Then the tip of the umbra reaches the earth. Sometimes the moon is farther away. The umbra does not quite reach the earth. And the moon does not wholly block out the sun. A person in line with the umbra sees a bright ring around the moon. This is an annular eclipse. *Annular* means "ring-shaped."

A solar eclipse is of great interest to astronomers. The sun is hard to study because of its bright glare. An eclipse, however, blocks out the glare. Astronomers can study the sun's corona—the outer layer of gases. It stands out as a fiery halo and can easily be photographed.

Astronomers never look directly at the sun, even during an eclipse, and neither should you. The sun's bright rays can damage the eyes.

OTHER KINDS OF ECLIPSE

The earth's shadow eclipses the moon. The moon eclipses the

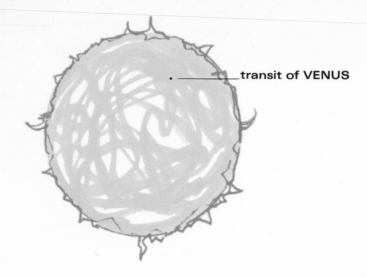

transit of **VENUS**

sun. These are the two best-known kinds of eclipse. But as seen from the earth there are many other kinds.

One planet may eclipse another. The moon eclipses planets. The moon and planets eclipse stars. There is a special name for these eclipses. They are called occultations. *Occultation* means "covering over" or "hiding."

Sometimes Mercury or Venus appears to cross the sun. The planet appears as a small black dot moving across the sun. This kind of eclipse is called a transit. *Transit* means "crossing."

Ecliptic *See* SEASONS
Elements *See* ATOMS

Ellipses An ellipse is a sort of flattened circle. It can be very flat and long. It can be nearly round. Or it can be somewhere in-between. The orbits of the planets are ellipses. So are the orbits of comets and meteors.

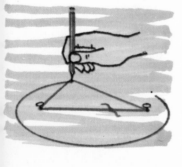

You can draw ellipses if you have: two tacks or sturdy pins; a soft board or a piece of thick cardboard; a piece of string about 10 inches long; a pencil.

Stick the tacks in the board. Knot the ends of the string together to form a loop. Place the loop over the tacks. Hold the pencil inside the string, pulling the string tight. Then move the pencil around, keeping the string tight. You have drawn an ellipse.

Move one tack farther from the other. Draw another ellipse. It is longer and flatter.

Move one tack close to the other. Draw an ellipse. It is nearly round.

The Andromeda galaxy.

Here is another way to think of ellipses. Look at the drawing of the cone. If you cut straight through a cone, you have a circle. If you cut through at a slant, you have an ellipse.

Equinoxes   *See* SEASONS
Fireballs   *See* METEORS

Galaxies   A galaxy is a vast "island" of stars in space. Our sun is a star in a galaxy called the Milky Way. There are some 100 billion stars in this galaxy. From one end to the other it measures about 100,000 light-years. (One light-year equals nearly 6 trillion miles.)

Telescopes show that there are millions of galaxies in space. Many are made up of billions of stars. Only three of these galaxies can be seen without a telescope. Two of them are seen in the Southern Hemisphere. They are called the Magellanic Clouds after Ferdinand Magellan, who saw them while exploring the Southern Hemisphere. The clouds are about 150,000 light-years away. They are the nearest galaxies. The other galaxy is seen from the Northern Hemisphere. It appears as a hazy patch in the constellation Andromeda.

This galaxy is sometimes called the Andromeda galaxy. That is because it looks as if it were part of the constellation. But it is not. The stars of Andromeda are part of our galaxy. The other galaxy lies far, far beyond our own. It is 2 million light-years away.

The galaxy is also called the Andromeda nebula. *Nebula* means "cloud." And at first that is what astronomers thought they were seeing. There are many huge clouds of gas in space. The hazy

A spiral galaxy.

patch seemed to be one of them. Then in 1924 a big, new telescope gave astronomers their first good look at the patch. It proved to be a galaxy of stars.

The same galaxy also has a third name. It is called M 31. That is a catalog number. Astronomers have made catalogs, or lists, of galaxies and nebulae. They often use a catalog number when speaking of a galaxy or nebula. The Andromeda galaxy is called M 31 because it is number 31 in the Messier catalog.

Another such listing is the New General Catalog. One of the galaxies in Pegasus, for example, is NGC 7479. (It can be seen only with a telescope.) It is never called the Pegasus galaxy. The reason is that there are three galaxies in Pegasus. The only way to keep them straight is to use their catalog numbers.

TYPES OF GALAXY

Astronomers divide the galaxies into four main types: spiral galaxies, elliptical galaxies, irregular galaxies, and dwarf galaxies. SPIRAL GALAXIES: Seen from above, our galaxy would look like a pinwheel. It is a glowing mass of stars and of huge clouds of dust and gas. Like a wheel, it turns around its center. Spiraling arms of stars trail from its edge.

Any galaxy with this shape is called a spiral galaxy. Most of the biggest galaxies are spirals. There are also smaller spiral galaxies. Seen from the side, a spiral galaxy looks like a wheel with a hub.

Some of these galaxies have a bright bar of dust and gas running through the middle of them. These are called barred spirals. ELLIPTICAL GALAXIES: Some of the brightest galaxies are the ones called elliptical galaxies. (An ellipse is a somewhat flattened circle.)

spiral galaxy

barred spiral galaxy

elliptical galaxy

irregular galaxy

A barred spiral galaxy.

These galaxies seem to be made mostly of stars. There is little dust or gas in them. They are smaller than spiral galaxies.

IRREGULAR GALAXIES: Some galaxies do not seem to have any special shape. So they are called irregular galaxies. All are made up of stars, dust, and gas. Both the Magellanic clouds are irregular galaxies.

DWARF GALAXIES: As the name tells you, dwarf galaxies are small. Some measure only a few hundred light-years across. They are made up of only a few thousand stars.

Some dwarf galaxies seem to be made only of stars. Others have dust and gas as well.

There are many, many dwarf galaxies in the universe.

GROUPS AND CLUSTERS

There are millions of galaxies in space. But they are not spread about evenly. Most are found in what astronomers call groups and clusters.

A group of galaxies usually has at least ten large galaxies. It also contains a number of dwarfs.

A cluster of galaxies is much bigger than a group. It may have several thousand large galaxies. It may have an even larger number of dwarf galaxies.

Our own galaxy is part of what astronomers call the local group. The Andromeda galaxy is at one end of it. Our own galaxy is at the other end—2 million light-years away.

The Andromeda galaxy is the biggest in the local group. Our galaxy is the second biggest. Both are spirals. The local group also contains another spiral galaxy, ten elliptical galaxies, and four irregular galaxies.

**Mass of dust and gas
in space shrinks and**

it begins to turn

A galaxy is formed

HOW GALAXIES DEVELOP

Huge masses of dust and gas are spread out in space. Astronomers think that a galaxy forms from one of these masses. The mass shrinks in on itself. It begins to turn. Spiraling arms trail out from the center part. Much later they close in on the center. All the time this is happening stars are forming out of the dust and gas. Finally all the dust and gas are used up.

If this idea is right, then the youngest galaxies are those with the most dust and gas. These are the irregular galaxies. The spiral galaxies must be older, for they have less dust and gas. The elliptical galaxies must be older still. They have almost no dust and gas.

Astronomers do not know how the dwarf galaxies fit into this picture. Some have dust and gas, and some do not.

See also: MILKY WAY; STARS; UNIVERSE

Giant Stars *See* STARS

**Gravity and
Gravitation**

If you trip, you fall to earth. If you throw a ball into the air, it rises and then falls to earth. If you shake a tree full of apples, apples fall to earth.

The apples, the ball, and you all fall for the same reason. The reason is a force called gravity. Gravity is a pull. Everything is pulled toward the center of the earth by gravity.

We are held to the earth's surface by gravity. Without gravity, the earth's spin would throw us into space.

The atmosphere is held captive by gravity. Without gravity, the

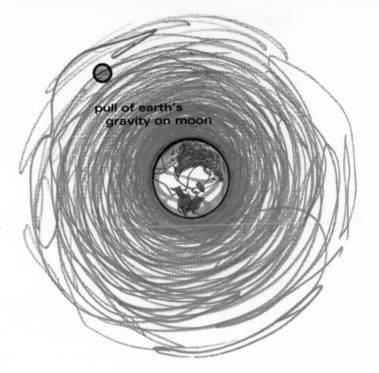

pull of earth's
gravity on moon

Earth's gravitational pull holds the moon in orbit.

gases in it would float away into space.

The moon is held in orbit by the earth's gravity. Without gravity, the moon would spin off into space.

The sun also has gravity. Its gravity holds the planets in orbit. In fact, every object, or body, in the universe has gravity. Even a speck of dust has gravity. The result is that every body pulls on every other body.

Sometimes this pull is very small. It is too small to be felt. For example, your gravity pulls on a ball. And the ball's gravity pulls on you. You do not feel the ball's pull. The ball does not move because of your pull. Still, the pulls are there.

In other cases, the pull is strong. The earth pulls on the moon. This pull keeps the moon in orbit. The moon pulls on the earth. The moon's pull is weaker than the earth's. But it affects the earth. It is the main cause of ocean tides.

The words "gravity" and "gravitation" describe the same pull. But scientists use the words in slightly different ways. They say "gravitation" when they mean the pull that every object has on every other object. They say "gravity" when they mean the pull of a planet or moon on an object at its surface. For example, the earth's gravity causes the ball and the apple to fall. Gravity holds you to the earth. But the pull between the earth and the moon is called gravitation.

The strength of gravitation depends on two things.

One is the distance between the two bodies. The other is the amount of matter in them.

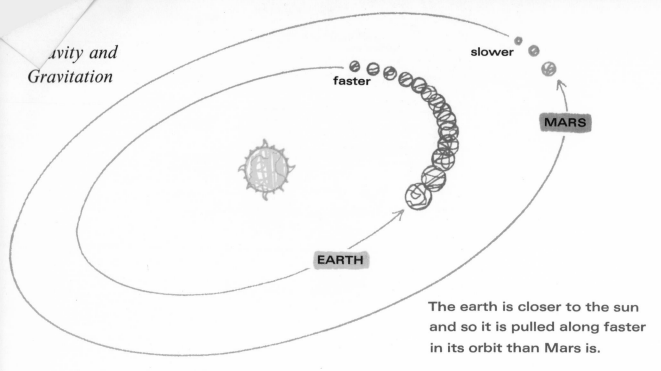

slower

faster

MARS

EARTH

The earth is closer to the sun
and so it is pulled along faster
in its orbit than Mars is.

Gravitation is stronger when the bodies are closer together. It is weaker when they are farther apart. For example, the earth moves faster in its orbit than Mars does. The reason is that the earth is closer to the sun. It is more strongly affected by the sun's gravitation. It is pulled along faster in its orbit than Mars is.

Every body is made of matter. Some bodies have more matter in them than others. There is more matter in an apple than in a tennis ball. There is more matter in the earth than in the moon. The more matter a body has, the stronger its gravitation is. That is why the earth holds the moon captive. That is why the sun holds the planets captive.

MASS AND WEIGHT

There is a word for the amount of matter in a body. The word is "mass." The earth's mass is greater than the moon's. An apple's mass is greater than the mass of a tennis ball.

Weight is the measure of the pull of gravity on mass. Suppose a person weighs 120 pounds. This means that gravity is pulling on his body with a force of 120 pounds.

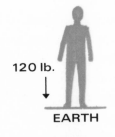

120 lb.

EARTH

Now suppose that person goes to the moon. His mass remains the same. That is, there is the same amount of matter in his body. But his weight changes. On the moon he will weigh 20 pounds. The reason is that the moon's gravity is about one sixth as strong as the earth's. The mass is the same, but the pull of gravity is weaker. The moon's gravity pulls on his body with a force of 20 pounds.

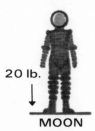

20 lb.

MOON

Inertia *See* SOLAR SYSTEM

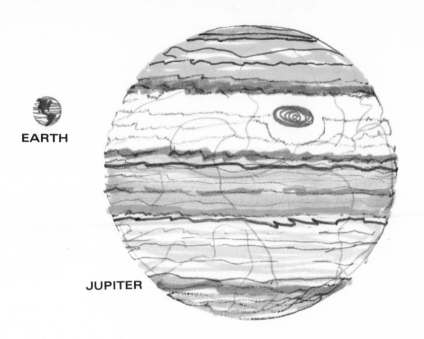

EARTH

JUPITER

Jupiter   The planet Jupiter was named for the greatest of the Roman gods. It was well named, for it is greatest of the planets. Jupiter is a giant planet, the biggest in the solar system. Its diameter is almost 11 times as large as the earth's.

Jupiter is the fifth planet out from the sun. It travels a bigger orbit than the earth's, and it travels more slowly. Jupiter takes nearly 12 earth years to orbit the sun once. But it spins very quickly. Jupiter turns once in just a little less than 10 earth hours. As a telescope shows, this rapid spinning gives Jupiter a slightly flattened shape.

A telescope also shows that Jupiter is a yellowish ball circled by bands of color. What we see, however, is not the surface of the planet. We see only the clouds at the top of the atmosphere. They reflect light brilliantly. That is why Jupiter is very bright in our night sky.

Jupiter's atmosphere is made of gases. Three of them are hydrogen, methane and ammonia. Astronomers think there must also be large amounts of helium in the atmosphere. The temperature at the top of the atmosphere is about −200 degrees Fahrenheit. Ammonia gas would be frozen at that temperature. So Jupiter's clouds are probably made of ammonia crystals. Perhaps snowflakes of solid ammonia fall on Jupiter's surface.

No one knows what that surface is like, for no one knows what lies beneath the clouds. Some scientists think that Jupiter has a core of solid hydrogen. Others think it has a core of rock about the size of the earth. The core may be covered with a deep ocean of frozen gases. Still other scientists think that Jupiter may be very hot beneath its atmosphere. Heat may come from the center of

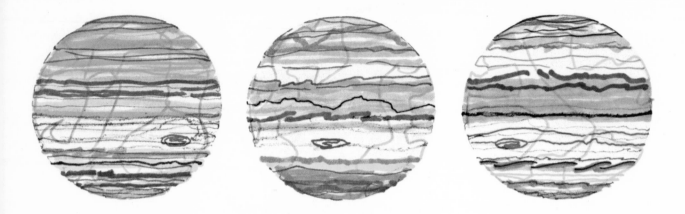

Jupiter's Red Spot

Jupiter. Heat from the sun may be trapped by the atmosphere. Perhaps the surface of Jupiter is covered with bubbling lava. Perhaps it is covered with warm oceans. No one knows.

Someday a space probe may tell us what Jupiter is like. But now all that we see is a cloudy, whirling ball. The atmosphere is thousands of miles deep.

The atmosphere is marked with bands of color several thousand miles wide. And the bands are marked by knots of clouds, storms, and other features.

The bands are always changing. They widen and narrow. They fade and darken. Their colors change to pink or tan or yellow or blue-green or gray. Sometimes a band disappears and then appears again.

A bright band of clouds circles the equator. Small storm clouds appear in it. These small, dark clouds are carried along by the wind.

To the south is another band of clouds. It ranges in color from yellow to light gray. In it is Jupiter's most famous marking. This is the Great Red Spot, which was first seen in 1665. The Red Spot is 30,000 miles long and 7,000 miles wide. It appears to float in the clouds.

Sometimes the Red Spot is easy to see. Sometimes it is almost invisible. Its color also changes. Over the years it has been brick red, pink, and pale gray.

Many astronomers think that the Red Spot is a solid object. It could, for example, be a huge lump of frozen ammonia. If so, it is a kind of floating island in the clouds. When it floats high, it is easy to see. When it floats low, it is hard to see. Other astronomers

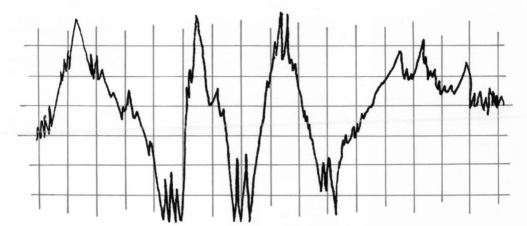

Record of radio waves from Jupiter.

think the Red Spot is a kind of giant storm. They think it is caused by something on the surface of Jupiter.

Jupiter's radio waves are still another puzzle. The planet sends out great bursts of very strong radio waves. They are picked up by radio telescopes on the earth. Radio astronomers are trying to find out just where the waves come from and why they are given off.

From what we know, Jupiter does not seem a likely place for life. And it is doubtful if men will land on Jupiter. The atmosphere is very cold. It may be full of violent storms. Jupiter's gravity is very strong. And the planet is surrounded by a sea of deadly radiation.

If men approach Jupiter, they will probably land on one of its moons. The moons would make a safer landing place. They would also be easier to blast-off from.

Jupiter has 12 moons. That is more than any other planet in the solar system. Four of them are very large.

Ganymede is the largest moon in the solar system. In fact, it is bigger than the planet Mercury. Ganymede looks something like Mars. It has polar icecaps. Its yellow-orange surface is marked with dark patches.

Jupiter's second largest moon is named Callisto. It is hard to see, because it reflects light poorly. Through a telescope it appears blue-gray.

Io is about the size of our moon. It seems to be a rocky ball. Some people see it as orange in color. Others see it as white or light yellow.

The fourth big moon is called Europa. Also about the size of our moon, it is light in color. Sometimes it seems to have icecaps at the poles and a dark belt at the equator.

Jupiter's four brightest moons in motion around their planet.

The other eight moons are much smaller. The largest has a diameter of 150 miles. The smallest is only 20 miles in diameter.

Four of these small moons are very far away from Jupiter. They orbit the planet at a distance of 13 to 14 million miles. The odd thing about them is that they travel from east to west. (The other moons orbit from west to east.) Astronomers think these four moons may once have been asteroids. Captured by Jupiter's gravity, they became moons.

JUPITER

average diameter	86,800 miles
average distance from sun	483,300,000 miles
average speed in orbit	29,400 miles an hour
time to make one orbit	11.9 earth years
time to spin once	almost 10 earth hours
temperature at top of atmosphere	−200° F.
moons	12: Only the four biggest—Ganymede, Callisto, Io and Europa—have official names. The others are usually referred to by Roman numerals, in order of discovery.

Light The sun and the stars are very hot balls of gas. They are so hot that they glow brightly. That is, they give off light of their own.

Any object that gives off light of its own is called a source of

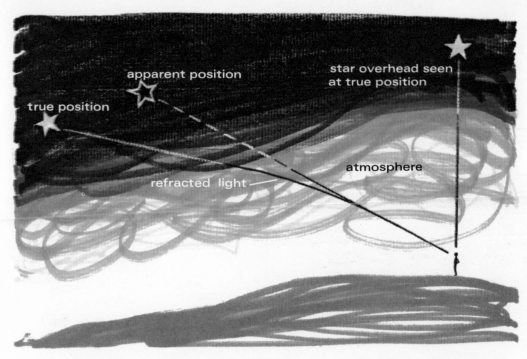

apparent position

star overhead seen
at true position

true position

refracted light

atmosphere

Starlight is bent, or refracted, by the earth's atmosphere.

light. Light spreads outward in all directions from a source. It travels in straight lines called rays.

When light travels in empty space, the rays keep the same direction. They also do this when light is traveling in material that is the same all the way through.

Sometimes, though, the rays change direction. They may, for example, bounce off an object and be thrown back. The throwing back is called reflection. The light itself is called reflected light.

The planets and the moon shine by reflected light. They reflect the light of the sun. That is the only reason you see them. Without sunlight they would be dark and invisible.

Light rays striking the moon are reflected, or bounced back. When rays strike certain other materials, they pass right through. For example, light rays pass through air, water, and glass. Sometimes the rays pass from one such material into another. Then they change their direction sharply. That is, they bend. This bending is called refraction.

Refraction takes place because one material is more dense than the other. That is, its particles are packed together more closely.

Refraction of light by air is important in astronomy. It means that things are not always where they appear to be. For example, starlight travels through space. Then it enters the earth's atmosphere. The atmosphere is more dense than space. And so the starlight is refracted, or bent. Seen from the earth, a star appears higher above the horizon than it really is.

See also: SPECTRUM; TELESCOPES

**Bending
of light rays
by water
and glass.**

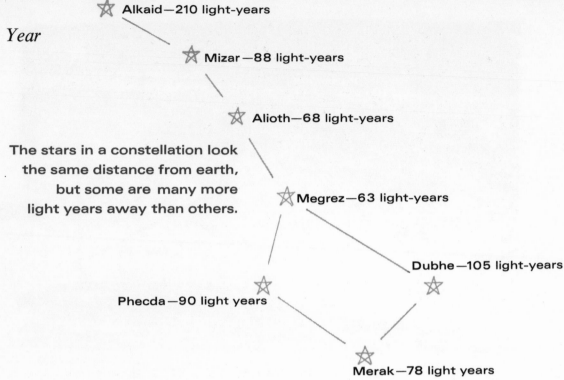

Alkaid—210 light-years

Mizar—88 light-years

Alioth—68 light-years

The stars in a constellation look the same distance from earth, but some are many more light years away than others.

Megrez—63 light-years

Dubhe—105 light-years

Phecda—90 light years

Merak—78 light years

Light-year The stars are very far away from us. The nearest star (other than the sun) is about 24 trillion miles away. Such large numbers are hard to talk about. They are even harder to work with. So astronomers do not measure the distance of stars in miles. They use other units of distance.

One of these is the light-year. A light-year is the distance that light travels in one year. Light travels very, very fast. It travels at a speed of 186,282 miles a second. In a year light travels 5,880,-000,000,000 miles. That is 5.88 trillion miles.

Suppose you read that a star is 300 light-years away. The figure tells you the distance of the star. And it tells you something else. It tells you that the light you are seeing started on its journey from the star 300 years ago.

Sometimes astronomers use an even bigger unit than the light-year. It is called the parsec. One parsec equals 3.26 light-years.

Magnitude *See* STARS

Mars Mars is one of the brightest objects in our night sky. It is also one of the most exciting. There is a chance that life exists on Mars. There cannot be people, animals, or big plants. But there may be very simple forms of hardy plant life.

This chance explains why Mars has been studied more than any other planet. Yet so far, the most interesting questions have no answers.

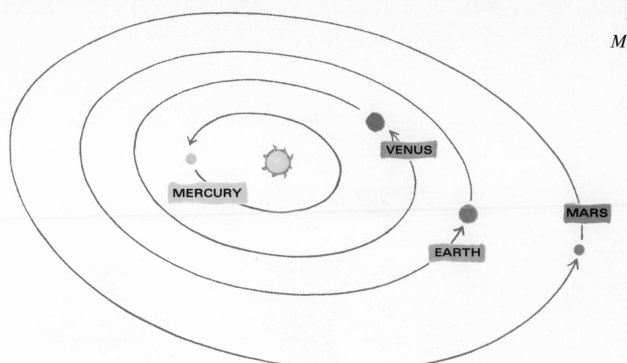

Mars is the fourth planet out from the sun, the next planet after the earth. Mars travels a larger orbit than the earth. And it travels more slowly. Mars takes 687 earth days to make one trip around the sun. A year on Mars is nearly twice as long as a year on the earth.

Being farther from the sun, Mars receives less heat than the earth does. Even so, it is much warmer than the outer planets. Like the earth, Mars is warmed by day and cooled by night. Its day and night last just a little longer than ours. Mars takes a little more than 24 hours to spin once on its axis.

Mars also has seasons. The axis of Mars is tilted much as the earth's is. Mars has the same seasons that we do, except that they last longer. On a warm summer day at the equator the temperature may reach 70 degrees. (But it may drop 180 degrees at night.)

Like the earth, Mars is a small, rocky planet with a thin atmosphere. But it is a smaller, lighter planet. Its diameter is about half that of the earth. And the planet is made of lighter rock. Its pull of gravity is much weaker than the earth's. And its atmosphere is much thinner.

Mars has two tiny moons. The larger one, Phobos, is about 10 miles in diameter. Its orbit is 3,700 miles above the surface of Mars. Phobos travels very quickly. A person on Mars would see Phobos rise and set three times a day. The other moon is called Deimos. It is half the size of Phobos and is about 12,500 miles from Mars. Seen from Mars, it would look more like a star than a

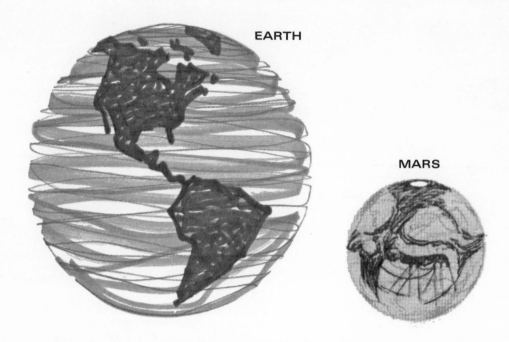

EARTH

MARS

moon. It is only a pinpoint of light in the Martian sky.

Nothing is known about the shape of these moons. Some astronomers think they may be asteroids that Mars captured. If so, the moons are probably big chunks of rock.

A telescope shows Mars as a fuzzy, reddish ball. The ball has markings on it. The markings are on the surface of Mars. Because Mars has a thin atmosphere, astronomers can see through it. They can see the surface of the planet. They can see that some of the markings change with the seasons—as plant life would. But they cannot see what these markings are. The reason is that our own atmosphere blurs their view. Looking through our atmosphere is like trying to see through running water.

Astronomers can see large, reddish regions. Some of them are dark red. Others are lighter—ranging from reddish to yellow-white. Sometimes a yellow veil sweeps over them. Astronomers think the reddish regions are deserts and the yellow veil is a sandstorm.

The reddish regions do not change from season to season. But the polar caps do. These are large, gleaming white areas. There is one at Mars's north pole and one at the south pole. In winter a polar cap grows and spreads. In spring it begins to shrink. By late summer it has almost vanished. In autumn it begins to grow and spread again. The polar caps seem to be coatings of frost, perhaps an inch thick.

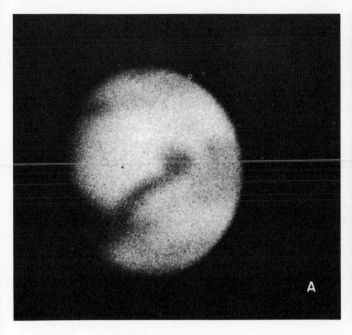
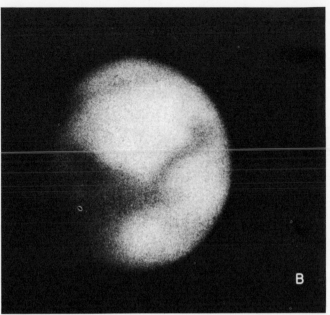

Photographs taken at Mount Wilson Observatory show Mars rotating.

Mar's polar caps grow larger in winter and shrink in spring.

The polar caps may be a sign of surface water on Mars. Also, water may be locked in the crust of the planet as frost or ice. Scientists think this is all the water that Mars can have. No one today thinks that the planet has lakes or oceans. Earlier astronomers did. They thought that the dark patches on Mars were bodies of water.

These patches are very interesting because they change. In general, they are big, dark patches hundreds of miles wide. Two kinds of change take place in them. The shape of a patch may change over a long period of time. It changes so much that it looks completely different. Then, later on, it may change back to its earlier shape. The patches also change color. Sometimes they look gray. At other times they look green. The color changes seem to take place over short periods of time.

Some astronomers say that the patches turn light green in spring. The light green darkens in summer. In autumn and winter the patches turn brown. Other astronomers say they have never seen these color changes.

Such color changes would very likely be a sign of plant life. But do they really take place? At present no one is sure. A telescope does not give the answer.

Within a few years a space probe will give the answer. One United States probe has already given scientists new facts about Mars. This was the space probe called Mariner IV. It passed Mars at a distance of 6,118 miles.

MARE CIMMERIUM

MARE SIRENUM
area in which photographs
at right were taken

Mariner radioed back photographs of one region on Mars. The photos surprised almost everyone. They showed the region to be pockmarked with craters. The crater walls slope gently. They are probably old craters, worn down by sandstorms.

Radio signals from Mariner passed through the Martian atmosphere. They showed that it is very, very thin. It is much thinner than anyone had thought. It seems to be made up chiefly of two gases, carbon dioxide and nitrogen.

Mariner also reported that Mars has almost no magnetic field. The earth acts as if it had a giant bar magnet inside. As a result, it is surrounded by a strong magnetic field. The field traps dangerous rays and particles that come from the sun and space. It keeps them from reaching the earth. These rays and particles must shower down on Mars.

Mariner's findings make life on Mars seem doubtful. But they have not settled the question. They do not, for example, tell us about the changes in the dark patches. If the patches are not plant life, then no one knows what they are or why they change.

Then, too, there is one other sign of life on Mars. New studies seem to show that there is methane in the planet's atmosphere. Methane is sometimes called marsh gas. On earth methane is made by bacteria that live in swamps.

Another fly-by probe may settle the question. Or we may have to wait for a space vehicle to land on Mars. The vehicle will put out a sticky "tongue." Or it may bore a hole in the ground. It will pull back samples of what it finds. Then it will run the samples

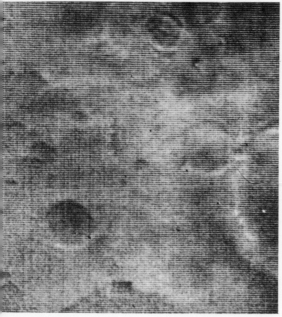
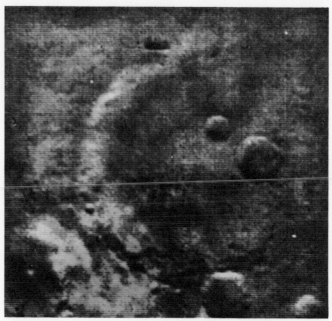

Mariner IV photographs, taken 6000 miles from Mars, show a region of the planet pocked with craters.

through special instruments. The results may finally tell us if there is life on Mars.

MARS	
average diameter	4,200 miles
average distance from sun	141,600,000 miles
average speed in orbit	54,200 miles an hour
time to make one orbit	687 earth days
time to spin once	24½ earth hours
temperature in summer at equator	
by day	70° F.
by night	−110° F.?
moons	2: Phobos, Deimos

Mass   *See* GRAVITY AND GRAVITATION
Matter   *See* ATOMS

Mercury   The planet Mercury is one of our fairly close neighbors. Yet little is known about it. The reason is that Mercury is hard to see. No one has ever had a really good look at it.

For one thing, it is a very small planet—the smallest in the solar system. Mercury is only a little bit bigger than our moon.

Then, too, Mercury is the planet closest to the sun. For us, Mercury is often lost in the sun's glare. It never crosses our night

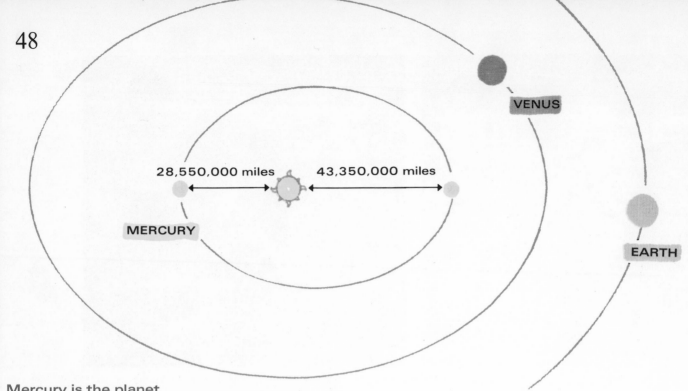

28,550,000 miles   43,350,000 miles

MERCURY

VENUS

EARTH

Mercury is the planet closest to the sun.

Mercury appears near the horizon in early evening and morning.

sky. We see Mercury only for short periods of time. Sometimes it appears near the horizon just after sunset. At other times it appears just before sunrise.

Like the earth, Mercury is a ball of rock. But it is a much smaller ball, and its pull of gravity is weaker. On Mercury you would weigh about a third of what you weigh here.

The earth is wrapped in an envelope of gases called the atmosphere. Mercury has almost no atmosphere. Long, long ago Mercury probably had an atmosphere and lost it. The gases boiled away in the sun's heat, for the planet's gravity was too weak to hold them. Today Mercury has just a trace of an atmosphere. It is very, very thin and made of a gas called carbon dioxide. It is not the kind of air that people could breathe.

An atmosphere acts as a shield against the sun. With almost no atmosphere, Mercury has no shield. It is bathed in deadly radiation from the sun.

Mercury probably looks something like the moon. Its surface must be bare and jagged and dry. No one thinks there could be any kind of life on Mercury.

Since it is the nearest planet to the sun, Mercury has the smallest orbit. It is also the swiftest planet. The sun's pull on it is greater than on any other planet. And so Mercury speeds around its small orbit. It takes 88 earth days to make one trip around the sun.

Astronomers long thought that Mercury also took 88 earth days to spin once on its axis. This meant that it always kept the same face toward the sun. The side facing the sun was a land of ever-

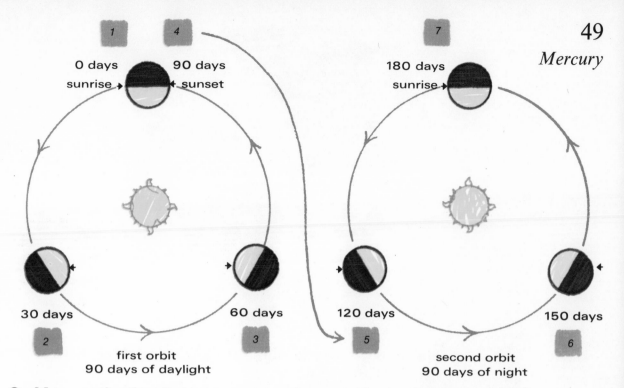

On Mercury the time between one sunrise and the next is 180 earth days.

day. The sun's heat blazed steadily on it. The ground was heated to more than 700 degrees Fahrenheit. The other side was a land of ever-night. It never saw the sun. Its heat—if there was any—trickled through the ground. Temperatures were about −450 degrees.

Today radio and radar astronomy have changed this picture.

Radio telescopes picked up radio waves from Mercury. Radio waves from a heated body give an idea of its temperature. The radio waves seemed to show that the dark side was much warmer than anyone had thought. There was only one way to explain this. Perhaps Mercury did not always keep the same face toward the sun. Perhaps it did not take 88 days to spin once. Perhaps every part of Mercury was being heated by the sun.

Powerful radar was turned on Mercury. It sent out bursts of radio signals. They bounced off Mercury and echoed back. The echoes were studied closely for clues to Mercury's spinning. Now astronomers think that Mercury spins once every $58\frac{1}{2}$ earth days.

Mercury, then, is not a planet of ever-day and ever-night. But days and nights on Mercury are long—the time between one sunrise and the next is 180 earth days. That surprises most people. But if you look at the drawings you will see how this can be so.

Each part of Mercury is heated and cooled every 180 days. During the long period of daylight, the ground becomes very hot. The sun is close and there is no atmosphere to cut off some of its rays. But the ground holds some heat during the long night. At night the ground temperature is probably about −10 degrees.

Mercury is not quite the terrible, small world it once seemed.

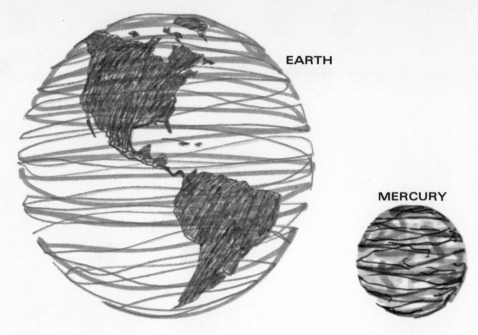

EARTH

MERCURY

Still, it is not very inviting. It is a close neighbor, but no one is likely to visit it soon.

See also: PHASES

MERCURY	
average diameter	2,900 miles
average distance from sun	35,960,000 miles
average speed in orbit	107,900 miles an hour
time to make one orbit	88 earth days
time to spin once	58½ earth days
ground temperature, night side	−10° F.
ground temperature, day side	?
moons	none

Meteors If you are outdoors at night, you may see a sudden streak of light in the sky. It flashes for an instant, then vanishes. Someone may say it is a shooting star. But it is not a star. What you have seen is a meteor.

A meteor is a bright streak in the sky. It is caused by an object called a meteoroid. A few meteoroids are large rocks. Most are tiny particles. They are the size of grains of sand or specks of dust. Almost every meteor you see is caused by a particle of dust.

How can we see a speck of dust in the sky? The answer is that we don't. What we see is its trail of glowing air.

All meteoroids come from space. They are objects that were orbiting the sun. We see them only if they enter the earth's atmosphere.

The Leonid meteor shower appears to come from the constellation Leo. It was very heavy in 1966, when this photograph was made.

Suppose a tiny dust particle rushes into the earth's atmosphere. It keeps hitting the atoms of the air. It hits them so hard that it jars loose their electrons. As the electrons join atoms again, they give off light. The air glows all along the path of the dust particle. That is the bright streak we see.

The trail is usually 50 or 60 miles above the earth. It vanishes when the dust particle does. Friction with the air makes the particle very hot. It burns up.

You can see some meteors almost any clear night. But there are times when you can see showers of meteors. These occur when the earth meets a great swarm of dust particles in space.

The particles are the remains of comets. They orbit the sun in the path the comet took. A meteor shower takes place when the earth crosses the path that a comet used to take.

Some meteor showers occur regularly every year. Each shower appears to be coming from a constellation. That is, it comes from the direction of a certain constellation, and is named for that constellation. For example, one shower looks as if it were coming from the constellation Perseus. It is called the Perseid shower. It takes place around August 12. The Orionid shower seems to be coming from Orion. It can be seen around October 20. The Geminids are seen around December 13. They seem to be coming from Gemini.

A great many tiny meteoroids enter the earth's atmosphere every day. Scientists say the number is between 90 million and 100 million.

From time to time a much bigger meteoroid arrives. It makes a

A very big, bright meteor is called a fireball.

brilliant flash of light. Sometimes the light is as bright or brighter than the brightest planets. Such meteors are called fireballs. A fireball may look like a round, glowing ball with a tail. (People sometimes think it must be a flying saucer.) Most fireballs burn up in the atmosphere. Only their dust drifts to earth.

Sometimes a really big meteoroid enters the atmosphere. It heats up, but it does not wholly burn up. It flashes through the sky and strikes the earth. A meteoroid that reaches the earth is called a meteorite.

A big meteorite strikes the earth like a bomb. On June 30, 1908, a giant meteorite struck northern Siberia. The shock was felt 500 miles away. The trees of a forest were felled for 40 miles in all directions.

Northern Arizona has the scar of a huge meteorite. It fell thousands of years ago and blasted a deep crater in the earth. The crater today is a mile wide and 600 feet deep.

Meteorites have been "bombing" the earth and moon for millions of years. They probably caused many of the moon's craters. (They probably also made the newly discovered craters on Mars.) On the airless moon, there is no wind and rain. There has been no weathering of the craters. On the earth, wind and water have worn down the craters. Only a few of the big ones can still be seen.

The Arizona meteorite crater

Long ago, scientists say, there were many big meteorites. Today there are only a few. Fortunately, they seem to fall in oceans or in areas where people do not live.

Most of the meteorites are probably asteroids. Asteroids are tiny planets. There is a belt of them between the orbits of Mars and Jupiter.

Meteorites are of great interest, for they are visitors from space. They are samples from another part of the solar system. And they are the only such samples that we have.

See also: ASTEROIDS; COMETS; TEKTITES

Milky Way   A hazy band of soft, white light arches across the night sky. To the ancient Greeks this band looked like a flow of milk. And so they named it the Galaxy, which means Milky Way.

You can see the Milky Way almost any clear night in the year. But the best time to see it is in late summer. Pick a clear night when there is no moon. Try to get away from streetlights and houselights. Then look up. There is the huge band of faintly glowing light.

If you have a pair of field glasses or a small telescope, take it along. It will show you that the hazy band is made up of countless faint stars.

THE MILKY WAY

There are billions of stars in the Milky Way. Astronomers think that there are about 100 billion stars in it. Along with the stars there are great clouds of dust and gas. These clouds are called nebulae. The nebulae hide many of the stars from view. Astronomers can see only about one tenth of the stars in the Milky Way. They study the others with radio telescopes, which pick up radio waves from distant objects.

The Milky Way is sometimes called the Galaxy. But it is not the only galaxy in the universe. There are millions of galaxies— each a huge "island" of stars.

Of all these galaxies the Milky Way is the most important to us. The reason is that we are part of it. Our sun is one of the stars in the Milky Way. So are all the other stars you can see.

At first this seems hard to understand. The Milky Way is a band in our sky. How can we be part of it?

Imagine that you are part of a huge crowd of people. The crowd is thickest at its center and thinnest near the edges. You are near one edge. Turn around and you see people wherever you look. But when you look toward the center you see the thickest group of people.

In the same way, the sun is part of a huge crowd of stars. It is near the edge of the crowd. We see stars all around us. Toward the center we see the thickest part of the crowd. This is the band of glowing light that is made up of countless stars.

Suppose you could stand off in space and look at the Milky Way. Seen from the side, it is shaped something like a huge pancake. The pancake is thick in the middle and thin at the sides. It is about 100,000 light-years long. (One light-year equals nearly 6

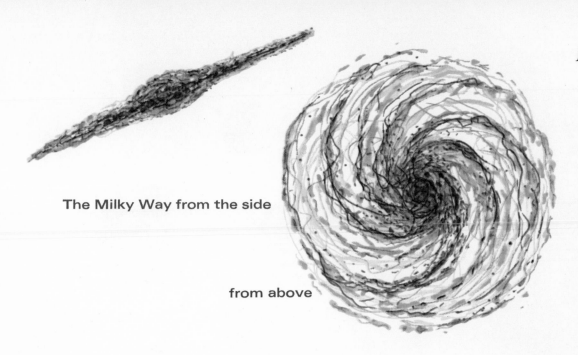

The Milky Way from the side

from above

trillion miles.) The middle part is about 20,000 light-years thick. The sun is in one of the thin parts. The thick part is the band we see in the sky.

Suppose you could look down on the Milky Way. From above, it looks like a pinwheel. The Milky Way has a spiral shape. At the center is a glowing hub of stars and gas. Spiraling arms of gas and stars trail behind the hub as it turns. The sun is in one of those arms.

The whole Galaxy is moving. The great island of stars, gases, and dust is turning around its center. The sun is moving along with the rest of the Galaxy. It is in one of the fastest-moving parts. The sun travels at a speed of about 140 miles a second. Yet the Galaxy is so big that the sun takes 200 million years to make one trip around the center.

See also: GALAXIES

Month *See* TIME

Moon The moon is our nearest neighbor in space. It is about a quarter of a million miles away. It is also fairly big. Its diameter is about one quarter of the earth's. And so the moon hangs large in our sky.

MOON

Astronomers can see the moon clearly. They have studied it closely. They have mapped its face. Over the years they have learned a good deal about it. Now they are suddenly learning much more. The United States and the Soviet Union are both exploring the moon by rocket. New facts are being added to those that astronomers had gathered from earth.

The moon is the earth's only natural satellite. A satellite is an

EARTH

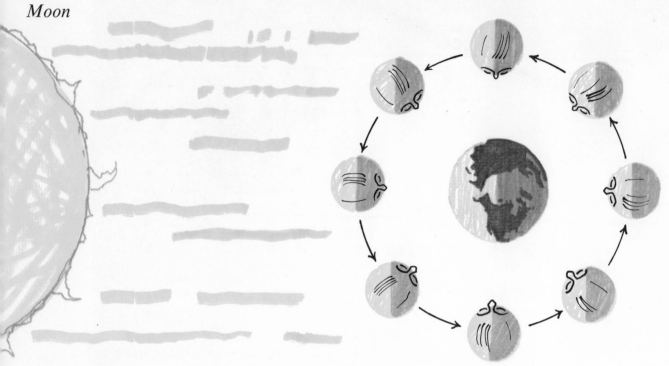

The moon always keeps the same face toward the earth.

crescent moon

full moon

gibbous moon

new moon

object that travels around a larger object. It is held captive by the larger object's gravitational pull. Some of the other planets also have natural satellites. These, too, are often called moons. But when people speak of "the moon," they mean the earth's moon.

The sun and other stars shine by their own light. The planets and their moons do not. They shine because they reflect the sun's light. The moon is a dark globe that is lighted by the sun.

Seen from the earth, the sun's light seems to spread across the face of the moon. We see a lighted sliver of the face. Night after night the sliver grows until we see the full face. Then less and less of the face is lighted. Finally the moon is dark, or new. These changes are called the phases of the moon. The moon goes through its phases in just a little less than a month. That is about the time that the moon takes to orbit the earth.

The moon orbits the earth. At the same time it is spinning on its axis. It takes the same time to spin once as it does to orbit once: 27 days, 7 hours, 43 minutes. As a result, the moon always keeps the same face toward the earth. The drawing at the top of the page shows you why this is so.

Until a few years ago no one had ever seen the far side of the moon. Now, United States and Soviet rockets have passed behind the moon. They sent back photographs. The photos showed that the far side is much like the side we see. It seems to be a little smoother. But it has mountains, plains, and craters, just as the near side does.

As far as we know, the moon is a small, dead world. A few scientists think that there may once have been life on the moon. Perhaps very simple forms of life existed there millions of years ago. If so, tiny simple forms of life may still exist on the moon. Bacteria, for example, might live in cracks. But the chance of life is very small. The moon is not a promising place for life.

It has little or no air. Some astronomers think that the moon has no atmosphere at all. Others think it may have a very, very thin atmosphere. Such an atmosphere would not be useful for man. He could not breathe it. It would not carry sound. It would not shield him from the sun's rays. It would not protect him from meteorites.

The moon has no surface water. Without air, there cannot be surface water. It would turn to vapor and float away into space.

With no air and no water, the moon has no weather. There are no winds. There are no clouds. Rain never falls on the moon.

But the moon does have a climate, and a terrible one. The moon is either blazing hot or icy cold.

With no air, the sun's rays fall directly on the moon's surface. The side facing the sun becomes very hot. The ground is heated to more than 250 degrees Fahrenheit. The hot day lasts two weeks. As the sun sets, a two-week night begins. Temperatures drop rapidly. The ground temperature reaches −260 degrees. The moon has a temperature range of more than 510 degrees.

The surface of the moon is rugged. The near side has ten great

Craters on the moon

mountain ranges and many single peaks. The peaks reach thousands of feet above the surface. Many of the peaks form rings around the big craters.

Craters are round, sunken areas. The smallest are pockmarks on the surface of the moon. Middle-sized craters are ringed by hills. The big craters—60 to 150 miles in diameter—are ringed by mountains. One of the largest craters is Clavius, near the moon's south pole. It is surrounded by a wall of mountains. Some of them are 17,000 feet high.

On the outside of a big crater, the mountain slopes are gentle. On the inside they drop off sharply. The crater floors may be very deep. Some are thousands of feet below the level of the plains. In some craters the floor is smooth. In others mountain peaks rise from the floor. Copernicus is one of these craters. Seven peaks rise from the center of its floor.

No one is sure how the craters formed. Some may have been formed by volcanic action. When the moon was young, rings of mountains may have pushed up. Then hot, liquid rock flowed out of cracks. It formed the floors of the craters.

Most of the craters are probably scars. They show where meteorites struck the moon. Long, long ago the solar system was full of huge rocks. The rocks traveled at great speed. And sometimes they crashed into the moon.

The moon is also marked by brilliant streaks. These are called rays. Rays reach out from some of the craters like spokes in a wheel. The crater Tycho has rays 1,500 miles long.

No one knows what the rays are. They may be cracks in the moon's surface. They may be dust, thrown out by meteorites. They

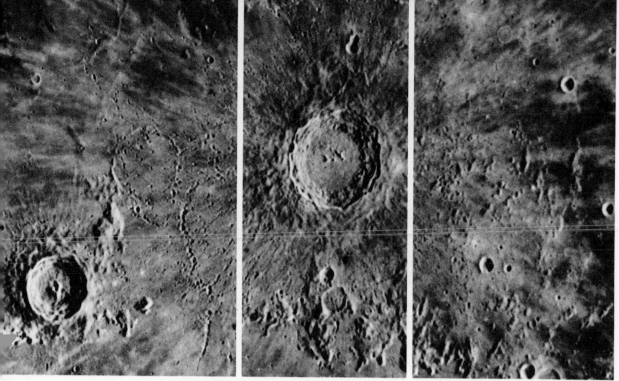

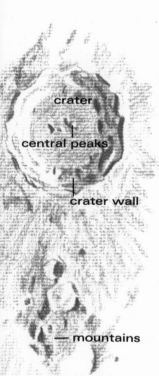

crater

central peaks

crater wall

— mountains

may be veins of rock.

The moon also has many deep rifts, called rills. These look something like deep, narrow valleys. No one knows how deep they are or what lies at the bottom of them.

For a long time scientists wondered what the surface of the moon was like. Was it firm and solid? Could a spacecraft land on it? Could an explorer walk on it? From the earth it was impossible to tell.

Now the first spacecraft have landed on the moon. The surface seems to be firm. The craft did not break through the crust. They were not swallowed up by a layer of fine, thick dust.

The surface of the moon seems to be gritty. It is strewn with pebbles and boulders. Parts of it are like a freshly plowed field. There is soft material. And there are clumps or clods of material. A space explorer would leave footprints. But he would not sink into the material.

These findings are very encouraging. They mean that the moon can be explored, first by spacecraft, then by men. They mean that many other questions will soon be answered:

Does the moon have a thin atmosphere? If so, where does it come from? Do the gases come from the sun? Or do they come from inside the moon?

What are the rays?

What are the rills like?

How did the craters form?

What are the dark areas known as seas?

Is there any life on the moon? Was there ever life on the moon?

And where did the moon itself come from? How did it form?

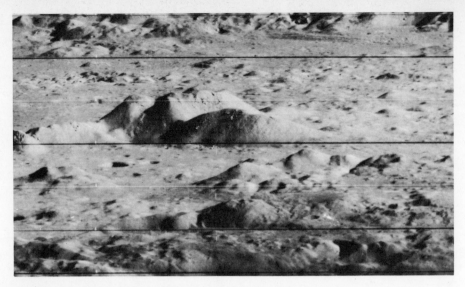

Part of the bottom of the crater Copernicus.

Those are just a few of the questions that scientists ask. Today they are questions without answers. Soon they will be questions with answers.

See also: ECLIPSES; PHASES; TIDES

THE MOON	
average diameter	2,160 miles
average distance from earth	238,854.7 miles
time to orbit the earth	27⅓ days
time to spin once	27⅓ days
surface temperature by day	250° F.
surface temperature by night	−260° F.

Nebulae A telescope shows that there are many hazy patches in the night sky. To earlier astronomers the patches all looked like clouds. And so they named the patches *nebulae,* which means "clouds" in Latin. (A single hazy patch is called a nebula.)

Modern instruments show that not all the patches are clouds. Some are distant galaxies—vast "islands" of stars. Some are supernovae—the remains of stars that exploded.

Others are clouds. They are huge clouds of dust and gas. Even without a telescope you can see one of these nebulae. It is in the constellation of Orion. It is above the bottom star in Orion's sword.

Nebulae give the Milky Way a blotchy look. Many of its stars are hidden from view by clouds of dust and gas.

Some nebulae glow with light. These clouds are found near bright stars. Others are dark. The dark clouds are sometimes called coal sacks. One of these is the Horse-head Nebula in Orion. Another is near Deneb in Cygnus.

Some nebulae form "smoke rings" around stars. These clouds are called planetary nebulae. Most are very faint, even when seen through a telescope. Only a few are bright and clear. One of these is the Ring Nebula in Lyra.

(above) The Horse-head Nebula in Orion.
(left) The Ring Nebula in Lyra.
(below) The Great Nebula in Orion.

Ⓒ

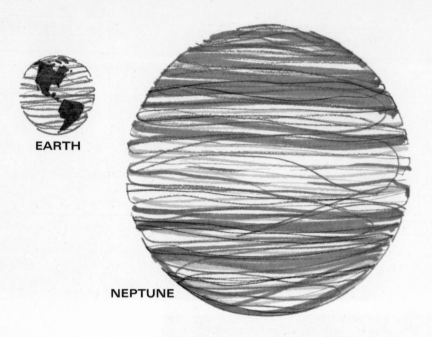

EARTH

NEPTUNE

Neptune   There are four giant planets in the solar system. They are Jupiter, Saturn, Uranus, and Neptune. Of these Neptune is farthest from the sun. It is the only one that cannot be seen without a telescope.

Jupiter and Saturn are big and bright in the sky. They have been known since ancient times. Uranus is a dim, greenish light. It was discovered only in 1781. Out of the discovery came the discovery of still another planet. This was a planet that no one had seen— Neptune.

Astronomers were plotting Uranus' path around the sun. They worked out tables showing where the planet would be in the sky. But between 1800 and 1820 Uranus behaved very oddly. It speeded up in orbit. Then it slowed down. It did not appear where astronomers expected it to be.

There had to be a reason for this. Perhaps there was another planet beyond Uranus. Its gravitational pull might affect Uranus. Suppose Uranus was overtaking this planet. Then Uranus would be pulled along faster in orbit. As Uranus moved ahead, the other planet would act as a brake. Uranus would slow down.

In the 1840's two astronomers attacked this problem. Each solved it by mathematics. They showed that there had to be another planet. In 1846 another astronomer found the planet. It was later named Neptune.

Neptune is nearly 3 billion miles from the sun. At that great distance it receives very little light. The telescope shows it as a dim, greenish object. It is circled by a few bands of color. Like the other giants, Neptune is wrapped in thick clouds that are made of gases. No one knows what lies beneath the clouds. The tempera-

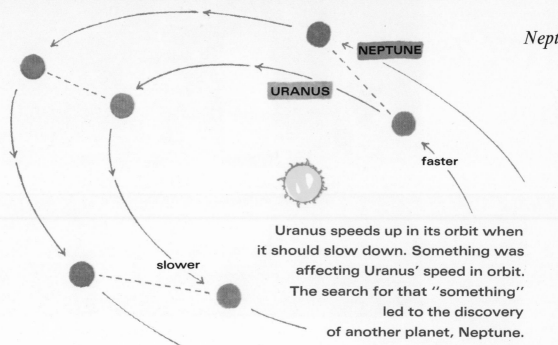

Uranus speeds up in its orbit when it should slow down. Something was affecting Uranus' speed in orbit. The search for that "something" led to the discovery of another planet, Neptune.

ture at the top of the clouds is about −330 degrees Fahrenheit. But astronomers think there is a warm region thousands of miles down in the atmosphere.

Neptune takes nearly 165 earth years to orbit the sun. Astronomers think that it spins once every 15 hours, 48 minutes. But they are not sure.

At least two moons orbit Neptune. The larger one is named Triton. It is a little bigger than our moon. It is as close to Neptune as our moon is to the earth. But Triton would look like a dull, gray disk. It receives very little light from the sun.

The smaller moon is called Nereid. It is only 200 miles in diameter. At its closest it is 1 million miles from Neptune. Sometimes its orbit carries it 6 million miles away.

NEPTUNE	
average diameter	28,000 miles
average distance from sun	2,794,000,000 miles
average speed in orbit	12,240 miles an hour
time to orbit once	164¾ earth years
time to spin once	15¾ earth hours
temperature in atmosphere	−330° F.
known moons	2: Triton, Nereid

200—inch reflecting telescope at Mount Palomar.

Observatories Astronomers study the heavens. They study the moon, the sun, the planets, the stars. They study great "islands" of stars, called galaxies. They study asteroids, comets, and meteors. Their subject is the universe.

An astronomer makes his studies in a place called an observatory. An observatory has telescopes, cameras, and other equipment. It has laboratories. It has a workshop for making special equipment.

It is easy to tell an observatory when you see one. It almost always has a round building. The rounded roof is called a dome. It houses a telescope. The telescope looks out through a slit in the dome. The dome turns, and so the telescope can face any part of the sky. When the telescope is not in use, the slit is closed.

Most domes are built on high ground. Sometimes they are built on the sides of mountains. The air is thinner and cleaner there; the view through the telescope is clearer. Many observatories are 1,000 or more feet above sea level. The highest observatory in the world is at Climax, Colorado. It is 11,300 feet above sea level. That is about two miles high.

At many observatories astronomers are studying stars. They are studying what stars are made of, how they shine, and how they change. Some of these studies are done at night and some during the day.

Working at night, an astronomer aims the telescope at the stars he wants to study. But he does not spend the night looking through the telescope. He spends it taking photographs. He uses the telescope as a giant camera. He records on film what the telescope sees.

Since the earth is turning, the stars seem to be moving. The telescope follows them. It is driven by an electric "clock." This is a

Inside the dome

motor that runs at a set speed. Even so, the astronomer must keep checking the stars. He does this through a finder—a small telescope that is attached to the big one. Then he guides the big telescope, keeping it aimed right.

The astronomer may take photographs for several nights. Then he begins to work by day. He develops his films. He studies and measures his photographs. He tries to work out what different facts mean. He may spend weeks studying photos that he took in a few nights.

An astronomer may make other kinds of studies. He may use a photometer to measure the brightness of stars. He may use a spectrograph. It breaks up the white light from stars into a rainbow of colors. Lines appearing in the colors are clues to what a star is made of.

Some observatories are equipped for special studies.

At one, astronomers may study the sun.

At another, they study radio waves. This is called a radio-astronomy observatory. Its telescope is not the kind you can look through. A radio telescope looks like a huge metal dish. It picks up radio waves from planets, stars, starlike objects, and galaxies. A radio telescope is not housed in a dome. It stands out in the open.

Almost every large country has a national observatory. In the United States, it is the Naval Observatory in Washington, D.C. A national observatory does several kinds of work. One of the most important is to keep track of time.

The observatory has clocks that keep nearly perfect time. But nearly perfect is not good enough. Astronomers keep checking the clocks against the stars. Certain stars appear due south at certain moments. Astronomers check the clocks against the appearance of the stars.

Solar telescope atop a 150-foot tower at Mount Wilson.

An orbiting observatory is checked before launching from Cape Kennedy.

A national observatory broadcasts time signals. In the United States signals go out over six special radio stations. They are picked up by ships and airplanes. They are picked up by the kind of radio stations you listen to. The radio stations set their clocks by these signals. Then they send out time signals of their own. That is how they give you the correct time.

Today there is a brand-new kind of observatory. It is an observatory that orbits in space beyond the earth's atmosphere.

The atmosphere blurs what astronomers see. It blocks certain kinds of radiations. Astronomers have long wanted to get outside the earth's atmosphere. An orbiting observatory makes this possible. The observatory is a satellite that carries instruments. The instruments gather information. The information is radioed back to the astronomers on earth.

See also: RADAR ASTRONOMY; RADIO ASTRONOMY; TELESCOPES

Opposition   Sometimes the sun is on one side of the earth. The moon is on the opposite side. At these times the moon is said to be in opposition. When the moon is in opposition, we see its face fully lighted.

Planets can also be in opposition. This is usually the best time for observing the planet. The planet shows us a fully lighted face. Rocket fly-bys are likely to be set for times when a planet is in opposition.

planets in opposition

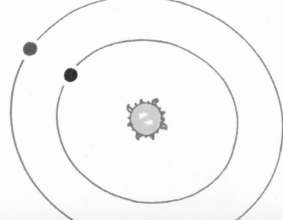

EARTH'S orbit

MOON'S orbit

Orbit   An orbit is a curved path. It is the curved path followed by one body as it travels around another body. The moon travels around the earth in an orbit. The planets travel around the sun in orbits. You can also use *orbit* as a verb. The moon orbits the earth. The planets orbit the sun.

Parallax   Hold a pencil at arm's length and look at it. Wink one eye. Then quickly wink the other. The pencil will seem to jump back and forth. The reason is that your eyes are set apart. One does not see the pencil just where the other does.

Now suppose an astronomer observes a star in June and again in December. By then the earth has moved from one side of its orbit to the far side. The two positions are like two eyes in the head. The star seems to have moved.

This seeming change is called parallax. Astronomers use it to measure the distance of stars. They can work out the distance by mathematics. That is how they have learned the distance of stars that are less than 300 light-years away. A star that is farther away does not seem to move.

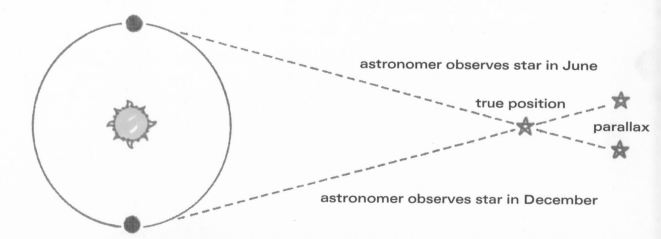

astronomer observes star in June

true position

parallax

astronomer observes star in December

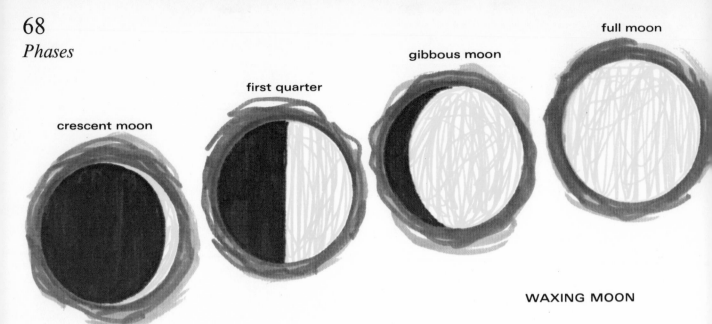

crescent moon

first quarter

gibbous moon

full moon

WAXING MOON

Phases The moon appears to change its shape. First you see a curved sliver of moon. As the nights pass, the sliver grows. You see a half-moon, then a full moon. After that you see less and less of the moon's face. Finally the moon is dark. Then a curved sliver appears again. These changes are called the phases of the moon. The moon takes just a little more than $29\frac{1}{2}$ days to go through its phases.

The moon does not shine by its own light. It shines because it reflects the sun's light. Suppose you could look at the moon from space. You would see that half of it is always lighted by the sun. Half of it is turned away from the sun and is dark. But it does not look this way from the earth.

Sometimes the moon is between the earth and sun. The side facing the earth is dark. This phase is called the new moon.

The moon moves on in its orbit around the earth. The side facing the earth begins to be lighted up. You see a curved sliver of the face. This phase is called the crescent moon.

Each night the sunlit part of the moon's face appears a little bigger. When you see a half-circle, the moon is in its first quarter. That is, it is one quarter of the way around its orbit.

The half-circle grows into a whole circle. When you see the whole face of the moon, the moon is full. Between first quarter and full moon, the phase is called gibbous.

At full moon the sun and moon are on opposite sides of the earth. That is why you see the face fully lighted. As the moon moves on in orbit, less and less of its face is seen. Its phases go from full moon to gibbous to last quarter.

From last quarter, the phases go to crescent and back to new moon.

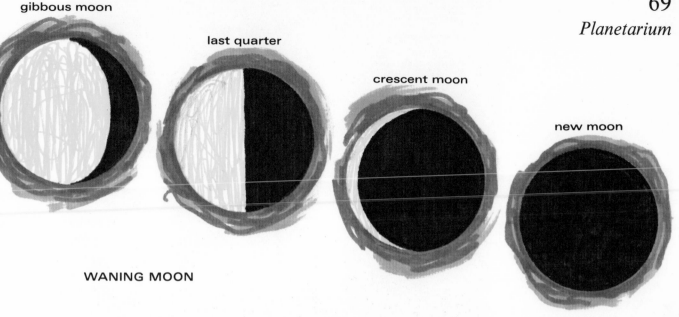

gibbous moon

last quarter

crescent moon

new moon

WANING MOON

Sometimes you hear people speak of the "waxing moon" or the "waning moon." The moon is waxing at the time when it is showing more and more of its face. It is waning when it is showing less and less of its face.

See also: EARTHLIGHT; MOON

PHASES OF MERCURY AND VENUS

Seen from the earth, two planets also go through phases. The two are Mercury and Venus. They are the two innermost planets. Their orbits lie between the earth's orbit and the sun. That is why we see them go through phases.

Sometimes, for example, Venus is between the earth and the sun. The side facing the sun is lighted. The side facing the earth is dark.

Venus orbits faster than the earth does. And so it "pulls ahead." We begin to see the sunlit side of Venus. At first we see a lighted sliver—Venus in crescent phase. The lighted face grows. When Venus is on the far side of the sun, the face is fully lighted. Then the lighted face grows smaller. Venus again overtakes the earth. And the dark side is turned toward us.

Mercury goes through the same phases, but they are hard to see.

Planetarium   A planetarium is a building with an indoor sky. On this sky you can see a moving picture of the stars, planets, and other heavenly bodies.

The indoor sky is a dome. It is shaped like an upside-down bowl. The inside of the "bowl" serves as a movie screen. A projector casts pictures of the sky on it.

The projector has the shape of a large dumbbell. The round part

A planetarium

at one end shows the stars of the Northern Hemisphere. The round part at the other end shows the stars of the Southern Hemisphere.

With the projector an astronomer can show you how the stars look from any place on earth—from San Francisco or Moscow or the South Pole. You can see how the moon and planets move among the stars. You can see how the stars seem to travel across the sky at night. The projector can show you how the sky looked at any time in the past. It can show you how the sky will look at any date in the future.

Sometimes the word *planetarium* is used for a moving model of the planets. Balls mounted on rods stand for the planets and their moons. When the works are set in motion, the balls move. The planets move around the sun, and the moons move around their planets. Such models were the first planetariums. Today one of these models is usually called an orrery rather than a planetarium.

Planetoids *See* ASTEROIDS

Planets Sometimes you see what looks like a wandering star. It is a slowly moving light that travels among the fixed stars. If you look very carefully, you see that this light is different in another way, too. The fixed stars shine with a twinkling light. The wandering star shines with a steadier light.

Astronomers of long ago knew five such wandering stars. The ancient Greeks had a special name for them. It meant "wanderers." From the Greek name comes our word *planets*.

Today we know that a planet is not a wandering star. It is a very different kind of body.

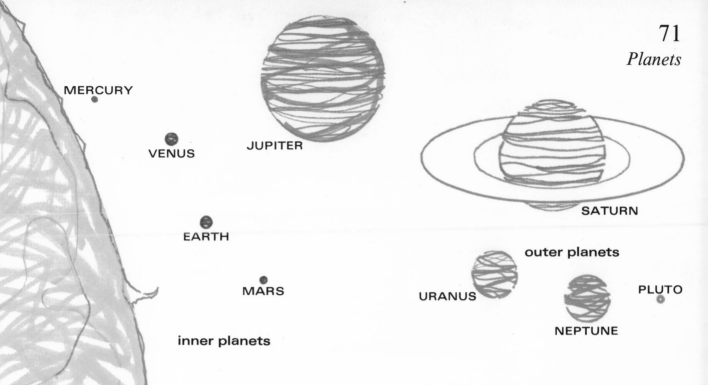

MERCURY

VENUS

JUPITER

SATURN

EARTH

outer planets

MARS

URANUS

PLUTO

NEPTUNE

inner planets

A star is a huge ball of fiery gases. It gives off heat and light.

A planet is a small, dark globe. It does not shine by its own light. It shines because it is reflecting light. The planets of our solar system reflect the sun's light. All of them move around the sun in orbits. As they orbit the sun, they spin. The side of a planet that faces the sun is lighted. The other side is dark.

Nine major planets orbit the sun. One of them is the earth. Five are the wandering stars of old: Mercury, Venus, Mars, Jupiter, and Saturn. The other three are Uranus, Neptune, and Pluto. Uranus can be seen without a telescope if you know exactly where to look for it. Neptune and Pluto cannot be seen without a telescope. In fact, Pluto can be seen only with a very powerful telescope.

There are also thousands of tiny planets in the solar system. These are called asteroids. The largest of them is only 500 miles in diameter. The asteroids also orbit the sun. Most of them are in the wide belt of space between the orbits of Mars and Jupiter.

There are two main kinds of major planet in the solar system. One kind is a small, rocky ball. The other is a giant with a thick atmosphere.

The four inner planets are small, rocky balls with thin atmospheres. These planets are Mercury, Venus, the earth, and Mars. Mercury has just a trace of an atmosphere. Mars has a little more. Venus has an atmosphere that is about 60 miles deep. Earth's atmosphere is even deeper.

Jupiter, Saturn, Uranus, and Neptune are the giant planets. Each is wrapped in an atmosphere thousands of miles deep. The top of the atmosphere is all we see of them.

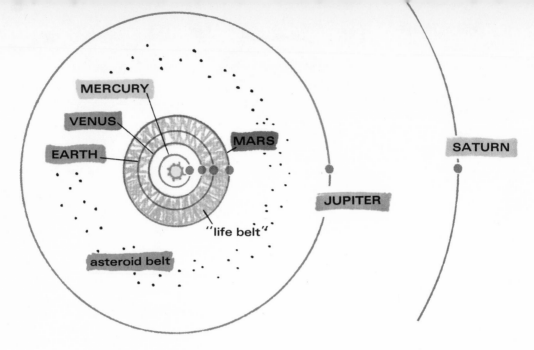

Pluto is the outermost planet. But it is not a giant. It is a small planet. Astronomers cannot see it very well, but they think it is a rocky ball. They also think it may once have been a moon that belonged to Neptune. Escaping, Pluto began to orbit the sun and so became a planet.

Three of the planets lie in what astronomers call the "life belt." This means that they receive the right amount of heat and light to support life. Venus, the earth, and Mars are these three planets. Mercury is too close to the sun for life. The other planets are too far away. As far as we know, there is life only on the earth. But simple forms of life might exist on Mars and Venus.

BIRTH OF THE PLANETS

Where did the planets come from? Many scientists think that the sun and the planets were born together. They think the solar system formed out of a huge cloud of dust and gas. This is what may have happened.

Billions of years ago a huge cloud of dust and gas was floating in space. Slowly the cloud began to stir. The particles of dust and gas

A huge cloud of dust and gas floated in space

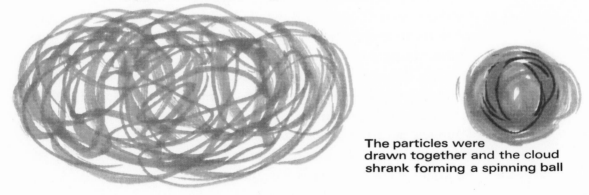

The particles were drawn together and the cloud shrank forming a spinning ball

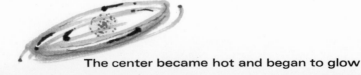

The center became hot and began to glow

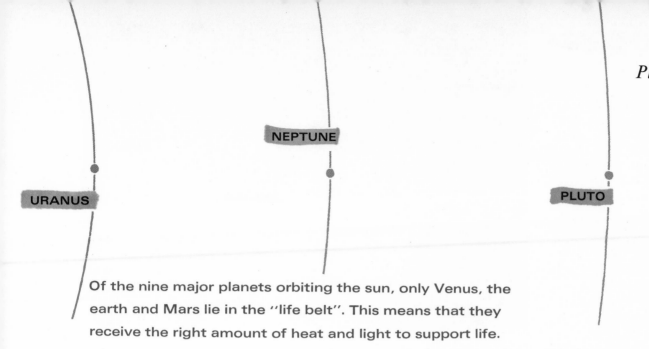

NEPTUNE

URANUS

PLUTO

Of the nine major planets orbiting the sun, only Venus, the earth and Mars lie in the "life belt". This means that they receive the right amount of heat and light to support life.

were being drawn toward one another. The cloud shrank in size. The particles moved faster and faster. And in time the cloud fell in on itself. It formed a huge ball and began to spin.

The spinning caused the ball to flatten somewhat. It became a big disk, thick in the center and thin at the edges. The thick center part was under very great pressure so it became extremely hot. It began to glow and to give off light and heat. The sun had come into being.

The outer parts of the disk were spinning very fast. They broke up into whirling masses of gas and dust. The particles of gas and dust were drawn together. In time these whirling masses became the planets. The planets were moving around the glowing ball that was the sun.

Each planet was wrapped in a thick envelope of gases. Radiation from the sun blew away some of the gases. The inner planets lost a large part of their gases. The outer planets lost only some of their gases. That is why they are still wrapped in thick atmospheres.

OTHER STARS, OTHER PLANETS

The sun is a star. It is a star with a family of planets.

Do other stars have planets? The answer is, "Probably." All stars are very likely born in the same way.

There are billions and billions of stars. Many of them may have planets. So there may be billions of planets.

We cannot even hope to see these planets, however. The stars are very far away from us. The stars are so far away that they are only points of light in our sky. Their planets must be invisible.

Yet astronomers think they have found three stars with planets. Each star seems to have an invisible companion. Each wobbles very slightly. The wobble is caused by the gravitational pull of the companion.

One of these stars is called Barnard's Star. It seems to have a planet 1½ times the size of Jupiter. The planet is 500 million miles from its star. That is about Jupiter's distance from the sun. But Barnard's Star is much less bright than the sun. Its planet must be a very cold place indeed.

Everyone wonders if there can be life on other planets. But that is a very big question. Scientists today can only guess at the answer. They say there may be life in other solar systems. But if there is, it may not be the kind of life we know on earth.

See also: ASTEROIDS; EARTH; JUPITER; MARS; MERCURY; MOON; NEPTUNE; PLUTO; SOLAR SYSTEM; URANUS; VENUS

Pluto The planet Pluto is a small, dark world. It is the ninth planet out from the sun. And it seems to be at the edge of the solar system. Its orbit is several billion miles from the sun. At that distance Pluto is a cold world of ever-night. The sun itself can be no more than a bright star in Pluto's sky.

From the earth Pluto is almost invisible. It can be seen only with a very strong telescope. Even then, it is small and dim. That is why Pluto was hard to find. Astronomers were sure that there was a ninth planet. They thought they knew where it was. But the search for this unknown planet spread over 25 years. This is how the search took place.

Astronomers had been plotting the orbits of Uranus and Neptune. These are the seventh and eighth planets out from the sun. But the two planets did not travel at their expected speeds. Something was affecting them. Astronomers began to wonder if that something was a ninth planet. Its gravitational pull might affect the movements of Uranus and Neptune.

An American astronomer set to work on the problem. His name

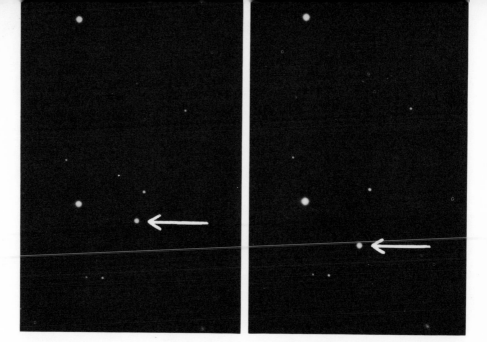

Photographs, taken 24 hours apart, show Pluto's motion among the stars.

was Percival Lowell. Working with mathematics, he set out to find Planet X. What size must the planet be? Where must it be in the sky? By 1905 Lowell had worked out the answers. He was looking for a small planet some 4 billion miles from the sun.

Lowell started to search for the planet. He knew that it would be very hard to see. It would appear only as a point of light. But it would move among the stars.

Lowell searched with a telescope and camera. He was looking for a "star" that moved. But the cameras of his time were not good enough. Lowell died without finding Planet X.

Later a young astronomer named Clyde Tombaugh took up the search. With telescope and camera he photographed a region of the sky. A few nights later he photographed the same region. Then he checked star against star in the photographs. He was looking for a point of light that had shifted. For a year he worked without success. But he kept on. In February, 1930, he found what he was looking for. He found a "star" that had moved. It proved to be the unknown planet.

The planet was later named Pluto, after the god of darkness. The name was a fine choice. The planet was a dark world. And the first two letters in its name were the initials of Percival Lowell.

The strongest telescopes show Pluto only as a dim, yellowish dot. Astronomers cannot even be sure of its size. They think it is about half the size of the earth. They cannot see any markings on the planet. They cannot see any moons. They guess that it spins once every 6½ earth days.

Pluto is probably a rocky planet. It may or may not have an atmosphere. If it does, the atmosphere must be frozen. Temperatures on Pluto are probably about −350 degrees Fahrenheit.

Very little is known for sure about Pluto. Astronomers know that

PLUTO

it is small. And they have plotted its orbit. They are certain of little else. Yet what they know shows that Pluto is a very strange planet.

It is more like the inner planets than the outer planets. The inner planets are small balls of rock. The outer planets are giants wrapped in thick atmospheres. Why isn't Pluto a giant?

Pluto is small. Yet it affects both Uranus and Neptune. How can it have such a strong gravitational pull?

Pluto's orbit is also odd. It has the shape of a long ellipse—a much flattened circle. Sometimes Pluto is closer to the sun than Neptune is. In fact, it sometimes swings inside Neptune's orbit.

Then, too, the orbit is out of line with those of the other planets. The others are more or less in line with one another. Pluto's is different.

Some astronomers think that Pluto was not born a planet. Perhaps it was once a moon that circled Neptune. The moon broke away from its planet. It began to orbit the sun and so became a planet itself.

That idea explains Pluto's small size and odd orbit. But it does not explain the pull on Uranus and Neptune. That is why some astronomers think there may be a tenth planet. Orbiting in the dark, it remains unseen by us.

	PLUTO	
average diameter	3,600 miles?
average distance from sun	3,670,000,000
average speed in orbit	10,800 miles an hour
time to orbit once	about 248 earth years
time to spin once	$6\frac{1}{2}$ earth days?
average temperature	−350° F.?
moons	?

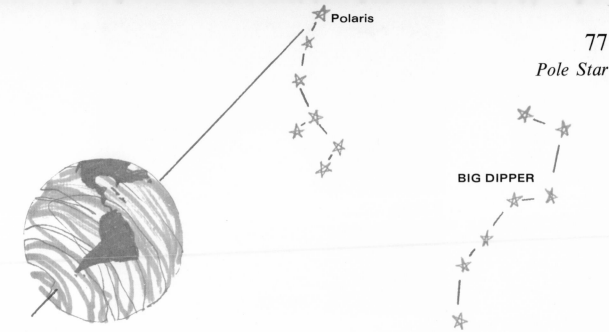

Polaris

BIG DIPPER

Pole Star If you need to find your way at night, you probably look for the Pole Star. Once you have found it, you know which way is north. The Pole Star is almost above the earth's North Pole. That is why it is also called the North Star.

Imagine a line from the earth's South Pole to its North Pole. Make the line continue into the sky. It points to the celestial north pole, which is the north pole of the heavens. The pole star is the brightest star near the celestial north pole.

Today's pole star is a star named Polaris. It is the tail star in the handle of the Little Dipper.

Polaris, however, has not always been the pole star. And it will not go on being the pole star. Over long periods of time different stars become the pole star. That happens because the spinning earth wobbles like a top.

As a top spins, its upper part slowly moves in a circle. The same thing happens with the earth. As the earth spins, the North Pole moves in a circle. (So, of course, does the South Pole.) It takes about 26,000 years to make one circle. The north celestial pole is also making a circle. And so it moves among the stars. The brightest star near it becomes the pole star.

Some 3,000 years ago Alpha Draconis was the pole star. By the year 7500 Alpha Cephei will be the pole star. And by the year 14,000 Vega, in Lyra, will be the pole star.

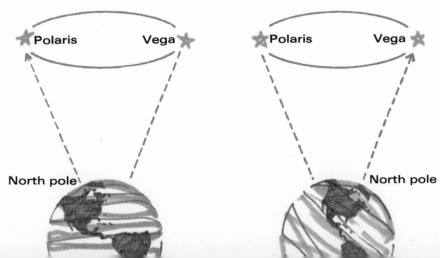

Polaris Vega Polaris Vega

North pole North pole

This quasar, 3C 237, is so bright that astronomers thought it was a star in our own galaxy. Actually, it is over 2 billion light years away.

Quasars A few years ago astronomers discovered some strange objects in space. They looked like stars. But they gave out tremendous quantities of energy in the form of radio waves. Each sent out billions of times more radio energy than any star could. The objects were named quasars. The name is short for quasi-stellar radio sources. (*Quasi-stellar* means "somewhat like a star." So a quasar is a starlike source of radio waves.)

Quasars also give off huge amounts of light energy. (Light and radio waves are different forms of the same kind of radiation.) In fact, they are the brightest objects in the universe. A quasar is unbelievably bright. One quasar may give off as much light as 100 galaxies each made up of 100 billion stars.

In photos quasars look dim. But that is because they are very far away. They are billions of light-years away.

Astronomers have found more than 100 quasars. And they have found many more quiet quasars. These objects do not give off radio waves. Otherwise they are just like quasars. They look like stars. They give off tremendous amounts of light. And they are billions of light-years away.

So far, quasars are a mystery in science. How can they be so small and yet so bright? How can they send out such huge amounts of radio energy? What are quasars?

No one can yet answer these questions. But quasars are of very great interest. Their energy started on its way to us billions of years ago. It started before the sun and planets came into being. It may have started when the universe began to take its present form. It may be a clue to the beginning of today's universe.

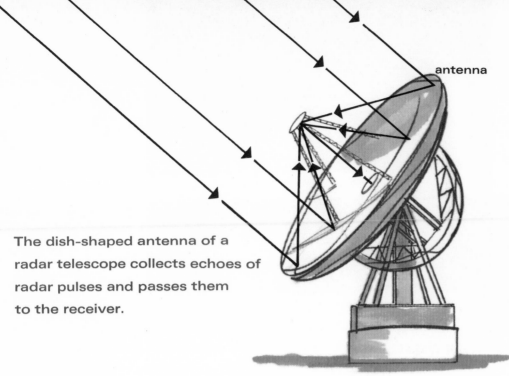

antenna

The dish-shaped antenna of a radar telescope collects echoes of radar pulses and passes them to the receiver.

Radar Astronomy

A radar set shoots out short bursts of radio waves. These short bursts are called pulses. When they hit an object, they bounce back, or echo. The echoes can be used to find out certain things about the object.

Radar was developed in World War II. It was used to find enemy planes. Radio pulses were sent skyward. If some hit a plane, they bounced back. The echoes showed as a "blip" on a radar screen. The timing of the echoes could be used to figure the distance of the plane.

Since the war, radar has been put to many peacetime uses. One of them is in astronomy. Astronomers use radar to study nearby bodies—the moon, the planets, the sun, and meteors. Such studies are called radar astronomy.

A radar astronomer uses a radar telescope. It has three main parts: a transmitter, an antenna, and a receiver. The transmitter produces pulses of radio waves. The antenna looks like a big dish. It sends the pulses out into space. It also collects the echoes. It passes them to the receiver. The receiver amplifies them (makes them stronger).

Radar echoes can be used to measure distance. They yield clues about the surface of an object. They tell something about its motions.

For example, the surface of Venus is hidden by clouds. No one has ever seen it. But radar has reached through the clouds. The echoes produced some surprises. One was that Venus spins backwards—from east to west. On Venus, the sun rises in the west and sets in the east. Another was the discovery of two big rough patches

Karl Jansky with his rotating radio antenna.

on the planet's surface. These may be mountain ranges.

Radar is used in studying the sun. The pulses bounce off the sun's corona, the outermost layer of gas. The echoes have helped astronomers measure the sun's distance. They have helped in studies of the corona, which keeps changing its size and shape.

Radar is also used to study meteoroids. Astronomers use it to map the paths of meteoroids that they cannot see. They can also measure the size and speed of meteoroids. Using radar, they have learned that swarms of meteoroids orbit the sun.

Radar can be used only to study nearby objects. It cannot be used to study the stars. They are too far away. Suppose, for example, a radar pulse was sent to the nearest star. It would take nine years to reach the star and echo back. Stars and other distant objects are often studied by radio astronomy.

Radio Astronomy

Where do radio waves come from? Most people would say from radio and TV stations. This is true, but it is only part of the answer. Radio waves come from many sources. They can come to us from electric razors and vacuum cleaners. They come from thunderstorms. And they come from the sun, the stars, and gases in space.

Many radio waves come from space. This discovery was made in the early 1930's. It was made by an American radio engineer named Karl Jansky.

Jansky was studying the crackling noises that are heard as static on radios. He found that some static was caused by radio waves given off by thunderstorms. But he heard strange hissing noises even when there were no thunderstorms. The strongest hissing seemed to come from around the center of the Milky Way. Jansky decided that the hissing must be caused by radio waves.

The Reber radio telescope.

Strangely, only one person seemed interested in Jansky's discovery. This was another American engineer named Grote Reber. He built a radio telescope. With it he scanned the skies for incoming radio waves. After many years he proved that Jansky was right. Radio waves are coming from the Milky Way.

The science of radio astronomy began with the work of Jansky and Reber.

Many kinds of radiation reach the earth. The atmosphere blocks some kinds. It lets other kinds through. Light is one form of radiation that passes through the atmosphere. Certain radio waves are another.

The length of radio waves from space is much shorter than the wavelengths of radio and TV broadcasting. Special receivers and antennas are needed for radio waves from space. These are called radio telescopes.

There are many kinds of radio telescope. Each has two main parts—an antenna and a radio receiver. The antenna may be a huge metal dish. The radio astronomer points it at the part of the sky he wishes to study. It gathers radio waves. The waves pass from the antenna to the receiver.

Radio waves from space are often weak. The receiver makes them stronger. It sends them to an instrument that changes them to electric pulses, or signals. The signals may go to a loudspeaker so that the astronomer can hear them. More often they are recorded on paper. A pen recorder is attached to the radio receiver. It records the signals as a wavy line.

Radio astronomers make many kinds of studies. For example, they may study the sun's corona—its outer layer of gases. The gases give off radio waves. And the waves make it possible to trace the corona.

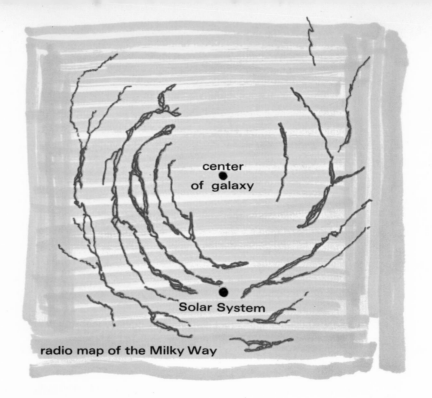

center
of galaxy

Solar System

radio map of the Milky Way

They show that it is very big indeed. We see the corona as a kind of halo around the sun. Photographs show it to be bigger than the eye can see. Radio astronomy has shown it to be bigger yet. Astronomers think that the corona stretches from the sun to the earth.

Radio waves from a planet tell something about the planet's temperature. Mercury is a good example. Astronomers had long thought that Mercury always kept the same face toward the sun. The day side of Mercury was blazing hot. The night side had little or no heat at all. Radio waves showed that this was not true. The dark side of Mercury was much warmer than anyone had thought. Later, radar studies showed that Mercury does not always keep the same face toward the sun. Every part of the planet gets some light and heat.

Radio astronomers are mapping the Milky Way. We see the Milky Way as a band of light in the sky. It is really a galaxy—a huge "island" of stars. The galaxy is also made of great clouds of dust and gas.

For many years astronomers tried to discover the size and shape of the galaxy. Dust and gases blocked their view. But dust and gases do not block radio waves. Astronomers have learned that the galaxy is shaped like a giant pinwheel.

The Milky Way contains many radio stars. A radio star is a source of radio waves. Like the sun, it may be a star that gives off light and radio waves. Or, it may be a star that gives off only radio waves and no light. Or, it may be the remains of a star that exploded. Or, it may be a cloud of gas. Anything in space that gives off radio waves is called a radio star.

Astronomers have found radio stars far beyond our own galaxy. Some of these radio sources can be seen. Others cannot. They can only be heard. So far no one knows what they are.

Radio Star   *See* RADIO ASTRONOMY
Radio Telescope   *See* RADIO ASTRONOMY

Satellites   A satellite is a body that orbits a larger body. It is held captive by the gravitational pull of the larger body.

The planets are satellites of the sun. The moon is a satellite of the earth. Five other planets also have moons, or satellites.

Planets and moons are natural satellites. They have been part of the solar system since it came into being. Today there are also many newcomers orbiting in space. These are man-made satellites. Each orbits a larger body and is held captive by it. Man-made satellites orbit the sun, the moon, the earth and other planets.

Man-made satellites are sent into space for many purposes.

Some send back information about the weather. They photograph clouds. They measure heat given off by the earth. They track storms.

Some satellites relay radio and TV signals over long distances. Some send out signals that are used by navigators. With these signals sailors and airmen can find their positions in all kinds of weather. Still other satellites send back information about the moon or a planet.

Most satellites carry only instruments. But some earth satellites carry men. These satellites are sent up and then brought back to earth. They are helping us learn what happens to the human body in space.

See also: GRAVITY; SOLAR SYSTEM

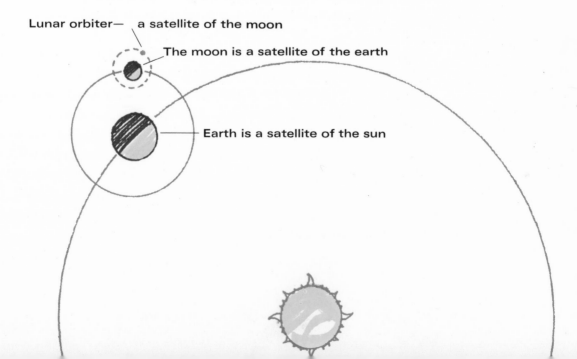

Lunar orbiter— a satellite of the moon

The moon is a satellite of the earth

Earth is a satellite of the sun

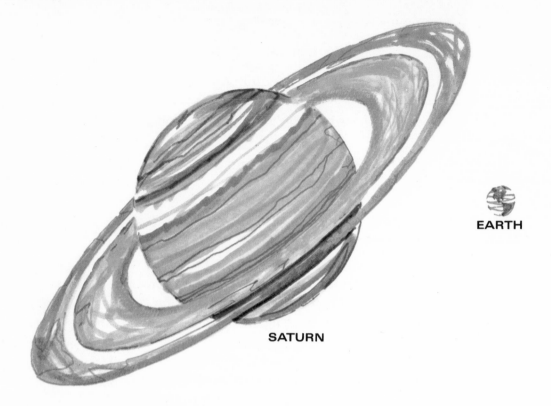

EARTH

SATURN

Saturn Saturn is the second largest planet in the solar system. Only its neighbor Jupiter is bigger. Saturn's diameter is about 9 times the size of the earth's.

Saturn is the sixth planet out from the sun. Traveling its long orbit, Saturn takes about $29\frac{1}{2}$ earth years to make one trip around the sun.

Saturn spins very quickly, though. It spins once every 10 earth hours. As a result of this rapid spinning, Saturn is slightly flattened at the poles. It bulges at the equator.

The big planet has a deep, thick atmosphere. The chief gases in it are hydrogen, methane, and ammonia. There is probably helium, too. Temperatures in the atmosphere are about −220 degrees Fahrenheit. Beneath the atmosphere there may be a layer of ice several thousand miles thick. Beneath the ice there may be a small, rocky core. Or the core of Saturn may be very hot. No one is sure. All we see of Saturn is the top of the atmosphere.

Bands of color circle the atmosphere. There is a yellowish band at the equator. At the poles there are greenish clouds. From time to time white spots appear among the clouds. These are probably lumps of frozen gases.

Saturn has at least ten moons. The largest is Titan. It is a giant moon about the size of the planet Mercury. Titan is the only moon known to have an atmosphere. Not much else is known about it. The big moon is very far away. A strong telescope shows it only as

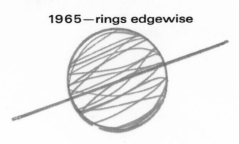

1965—rings edgewise

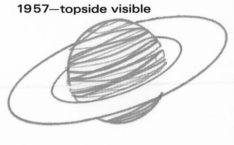

1957—topside visible

1972—underside visible

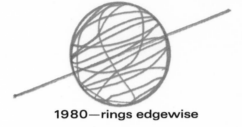

1980—rings edgewise

a yellow-orange object with two dark patches.

Saturn's outermost moon is called Phoebe. It orbits Saturn from east to west. The other moons orbit their planet from west to east. Phoebe may be an asteroid that Saturn captured.

In many ways Saturn is like Jupiter. But there is one thing that makes Saturn different from Jupiter and every other planet. Saturn alone is circled by flat rings. The rings make Saturn one of the most beautiful objects in the sky. (You need a good telescope to see them well.)

The rings lie one inside another. Nearest Saturn there is a darkish inner ring. Next comes a broad bright ring. Then there is a small gap. Finally there is the outer ring, which is also darkish. Together the rings spread out some 41,000 miles from the planet. They are only about 10 miles thick, though. When they face us edge-on, we cannot see them at all.

The rings are made up of billions of tiny particles. Some are as small as specks of dust. Others are the size of baseballs. Each travels around Saturn in its own orbit.

The particles reflect light well. This probably means they are icy.

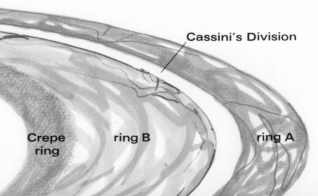

Cassini's Division

Crepe ring **ring B** **ring A**

No one knows how Saturn's rings formed. They may be the remains of a moon that broke up.

Some may be snowballs of ice crystals. Others may be tiny pieces of rock covered with ice.

No one is sure why Saturn has rings. The rings may be material left over from the time Saturn formed. They may be the remains of a moon. Or they may be something else.

SATURN	
average diameter	71,500 miles
average distance from sun	886,200,000 miles
average speed in orbit	21,700 miles an hour
time to make one orbit	29½ earth years
time to spin once	about 10 earth hours
temperature in atmosphere	−220° F.
moons	10 known: Janus, Mimas, Enceladus, Tethys, Dione, Rhea, Titan, Hyperion, Iapetus, Phoebe.

Seasons As the earth travels around the sun, the seasons change. Each year winter becomes spring and spring becomes summer. Summer changes into autumn and autumn into winter. We mark the changing seasons in two ways. We feel a change in temperature—the days grow warmer or cooler. We see a change in daylight—the length of day grows longer or shorter.

We cannot see the earth in orbit. But these changes tell us something about what is happening. During part of the year the North

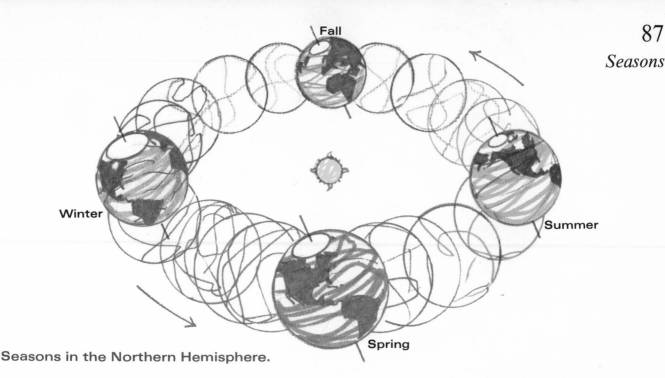

Seasons in the Northern Hemisphere.

Pole is tipped toward the sun; the South Pole is tipped away. During another part of the year the North Pole is tipped away from the sun; the South Pole is tipped toward it. When it is summer in the north, it is winter in the south.

It is summer in the Northern Hemisphere when the North Pole is tipped toward the sun. The sun appears high in the sky. It shines for many hours each day. In the far north it shines for 24 hours a day.

As summer passes, the North Pole is being carried slowly away from the sun. The days grow shorter. The sun appears lower in the sky at noon. Summer turns into autumn and autumn into winter. In winter the sun shines for only a few hours each day. And it is always low in the sky. The North Pole is tipped away from the sun. In the far north the sun does not rise at all.

As the North Pole is slowly carried toward the sun, winter passes. Days grow longer. The sun appears higher in the sky. Spring has come.

Only one part of the earth does not have seasons. This is the region near the equator. It receives the same amount of sunlight all year long. The only season it knows is summer.

WHY ONE SEASON IS WARMER THAN ANOTHER

The warmth of a season depends on two things. One is the strength of the sun's rays. The other is the number of hours that the sun shines each day.

In summer the sun is high overhead. Its rays fall directly on the ground, and so they are strong. Also, the sun shines for many hours each day. Its strong rays have lots of time to heat up the earth.

Slanted rays spread out over a greater area.

In winter the sun is low in the sky. Its rays reach the ground at a slant. The rays are spread out over a greater area, and they are not so strong. The sun shines for fewer hours each day. The weaker rays do not have much time to heat up the earth.

WHEN THE SEASONS BEGIN

We know that the earth moves around the sun. But that is not the way things look to us. As we see it, the earth seems to stand still. The sun seems to move around the earth.

Sometimes astronomers find it useful to pretend that the sun does move around the earth. For example, they find this useful when they are working out the seasons.

They pretend that the earth is at the center of a hollow globe. They have a name for the inside of the globe. It is called the celestial (heavenly) sphere. The sun's path forms a circle on the inside of the sphere. This path is called the ecliptic. The sun takes a year to travel around the ecliptic.

The earth's axis is an imaginary line that runs from pole to pole through the center of the earth. Imagine the axis made much longer. It will touch the celestial sphere at two points. These are the celestial poles. Halfway between them is another circle. It is called the celestial equator.

Look at the drawing that shows the celestial sphere. Trace the ecliptic, which is the sun's path. You will see that it crosses the celestial equator at point A. When the sun reaches point A, it appears to us to lie on the celestial equator. Its light "cuts" the earth in half, from pole to pole. At this time day and night are the same length in nearly every part of the earth. Astronomers say that the sun is at equinox. *Equinox* means "equal night."

Go on tracing the ecliptic. Follow it as the sun moves north of the celestial equator. The most northern point is marked B. At

celestial sphere

ecliptic

north celestial pole

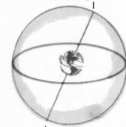

south celestial pole

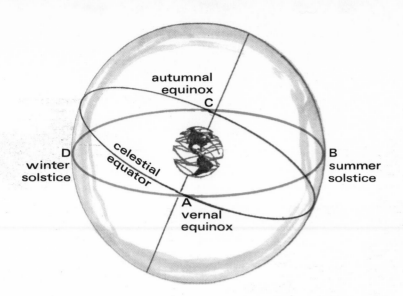

this point the sun appears to stand still for a moment. Point B marks a solstice. *Solstice* comes from Latin words meaning "sun stands still."

After the solstice the sun begins to move south. It again crosses the celestial equator, at point C. A second equinox takes place.

The sun goes on moving southward. The most southern point of the ecliptic is at point D. Here the sun again appears to stand still. Point D is a second solstice. After passing the solstice, the sun heads north again.

The equinoxes and the solstices mark the beginning of the seasons.

In the Northern Hemisphere spring begins when the sun reaches the equinox at A. This is the vernal, or spring, equinox. It comes around March 21.

The sun goes on moving north. It appears higher and higher in the sky. It shines longer and longer.

Around June 22 the sun reaches the summer solstice at B. The sun is at its highest point in the sky. It shines for the longest time. The summer solstice is the longest day in the year. It marks the beginning of summer.

The sun then begins to move south. Days are still long, but they are growing shorter. Around September 23 the sun again crosses the celestial equator. The autumnal equinox takes place.

The sun goes on moving south. Now days are shorter than nights. They grow shorter and shorter as the sun moves along the ecliptic. Around December 22 the sun reaches point D. This is the winter solstice and the shortest day of the year.

Winter has begun. The sun is low in the sky. The days are short, but they are growing longer. The sun is moving toward the spring equinox.

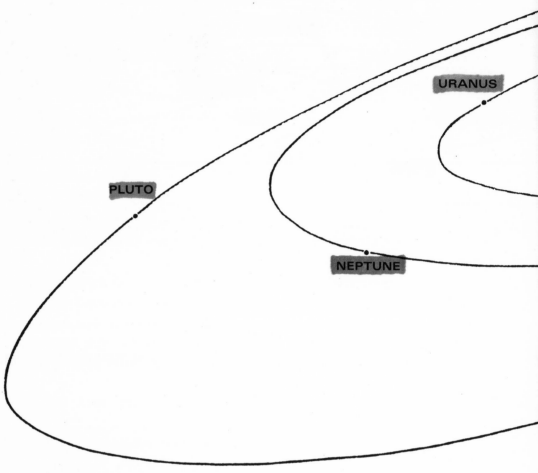

Shooting Stars   *See* METEORS

Solar System   The sun and its family form our solar system. The planets and their moons are members of the family. So are comets and meteoroids. All of them travel around the sun. All are held captive by the sun.

The word *solar* means "of the sun." So the solar system is the system of the sun. The sun is at the heart of the system. The members of the family move around the sun. They move around it in paths called orbits.

Nine major planets orbit the sun. They are: Mercury, Venus, the earth, Mars, Jupiter, Saturn, Uranus, Neptune, and Pluto. Between the orbits of Mars and Jupiter there is a belt of tiny planets. They are called asteroids. There are thousands of asteroids, and they are all very small. The largest is only 500 miles in diameter.

Wide gaps of space separate the orbits of the planets. The gaps grow bigger as you move outward in the solar system. For ex-

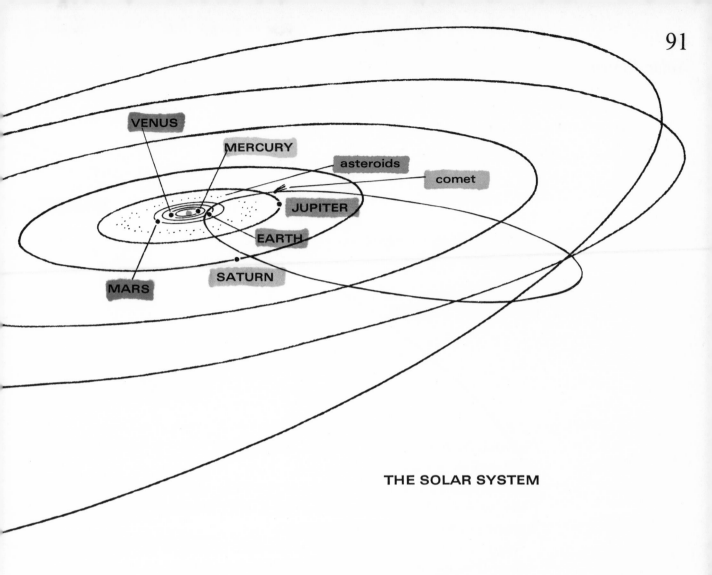

VENUS

MERCURY

asteroids

comet

JUPITER

EARTH

SATURN

MARS

THE SOLAR SYSTEM

91

ample, the earth is the third planet out from the sun and Pluto is
the ninth. But Pluto is 40 times farther from the sun than the
earth is.

The solar system seems very big to us. Mercury, the innermost
planet, is about 36 million miles from the sun. The earth is 93
million miles from the sun. Pluto is sometimes 4 billion miles from
the sun. Suppose you wanted to make a scale model of the solar
system. You let a ping-pong ball stand for the earth. Then Pluto
must be placed 10 miles away.

The orbits of the planets have the shapes of ellipses. An ellipse
is a somewhat flattened circle. It can be long and flat, like a cigar;
many comets travel cigar-shaped orbits. It can be nearly round;
the earth's orbit is nearly a circle. Or it can be somewhere in-between.

If the orbits were circles, each planet would always be the same
distance from the sun. But the orbits are ellipses, and the sun is
closer to one end than the other. This means that a planet's distance from the sun changes. In early January, for example, the

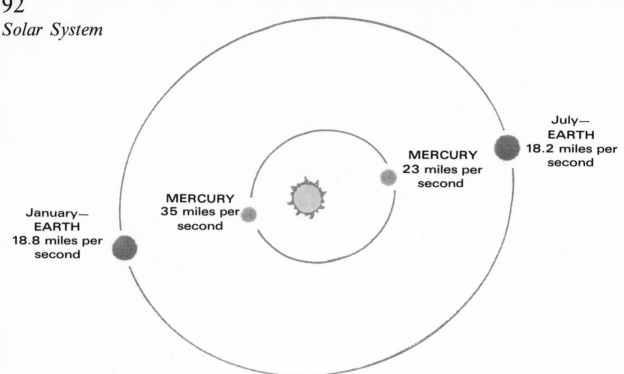

earth is 91,400,000 miles from the sun. In early July it is 94,400,000 miles from the sun.

A planet moves fastest when it is closest to the sun. In January the earth is orbiting at a speed of 18.8 miles a second. In July its speed in orbit is 18.2 miles a second.

No two planets orbit the sun at the same speeds. The closer an orbit is to the sun, the faster the planet moves. Mercury's orbit is closest to the sun. Mercury is the fastest-moving planet. Venus moves a little more slowly than Mercury. The earth moves more slowly than Venus, and so on. Pluto's speed in orbit is about one tenth of Mercury's.

A planet orbits the sun because two forces are acting on it. One is a force called inertia. The other is the sun's gravitation, or pull.

Perhaps the best way to understand inertia is to think of a ball. Suppose the ball is lying on the ground. It will simply lie there. It will not move unless it is acted on by some outside force. It may move if the wind blows hard. It will move if you give it a push. You can sum this up by saying: An object at rest tends to remain at rest unless acted upon by some outside force.

Suppose you do give the ball a push. It rolls. After a while it stops rolling. It stops because of friction with the ground. Without friction, the ball would roll on and on in a straight line. It would roll forever unless something blocked its way. You can sum this up by saying: An object in motion tends to remain in motion unless acted upon by some outside force.

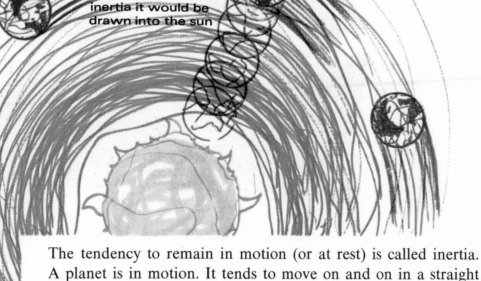

Without the sun's gravitational pull the earth would move off into space

Without the earth's inertia it would be drawn into the sun

The tendency to remain in motion (or at rest) is called inertia.

A planet is in motion. It tends to move on and on in a straight line. But it is acted on by an outside force. That force is the sun's gravitation. It pulls the planet toward the sun.

Without the sun's gravitation, the planet would move straight off into space. Without inertia, it would be drawn into the sun. As it is, the two forces balance each other. The planet moves around the sun in a curved path.

An inner planet is closer to the sun. It is pulled toward the sun with more force than an outer planet. That is why it moves faster than an outer planet. And that is why a planet moves fastest in orbit when it is closest to the sun.

See also: ASTEROIDS; COMETS; EARTH; GRAVITY AND GRAVITATION; JUPITER; MARS; MERCURY; METEORS; MOON; NEPTUNE; PLANETS; PLUTO; SUN; URANUS; VENUS

Solar Wind   The solar (sun) wind is a discovery of the space age. Space probes have shown that a wind "blows" steadily from the sun. The solar wind, however, is not like any wind that we know on earth. It is a flow of gas particles that carry an electric charge.

The solar wind comes from the sun's atmosphere. The outer part of the atmosphere is called the corona. It forms a soft halo around the sun. The solar wind is really the corona, which is moving out from the sun in all directions.

Solstice   *See* SEASONS

Spectrum Light from a very hot source is called white light. White light comes to us from the sun and stars. It is a mixture of colors. And it can be broken up into those colors. You see proof of that every time you see a rainbow. White light from the sun is broken up by drops of water in the air. It spreads into a rainbow of red, orange, yellow, green, blue, and violet.

Sometimes you see these colors when sunlight strikes a window in a certain way. You can make the colors appear if you have a prism. A prism is a piece of glass in the shape of a solid triangle. When white light passes through a prism, it is bent and spread out into its colors. The band of colors is called a spectrum. (The plural of spectrum is *spectra*.)

That fact is very useful to astronomers. With a telescope they gather light from a star. They pass the light through an instrument called a spectroscope. It spreads the light into a spectrum. Usually the spectroscope is fitted with a camera that photographs spectra. Together, a spectroscope and a camera are called a spectrograph. The photo is called a spectrogram.

When the colors of a spectrum are widely spread, thousands of lines can be seen in them. Some lines are dark; others are bright. By studying these lines, astronomers can tell what chemical elements are present in the light source. No two elements have the same pattern of lines. Helium has one pattern and hydrogen another. Oxygen has a pattern, and so does calcium. That is how astronomers discover what stars are made of.

The lines also tell whether a light source is moving toward the earth or away from the earth. Sometimes lines in a spectrum are

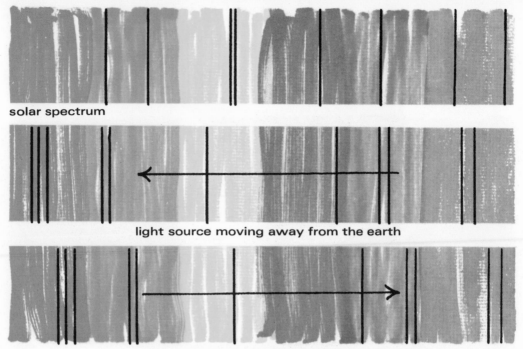

solar spectrum

light source moving away from the earth

light source moving toward the earth

shifted toward the red end. That means the light source is moving away. Sometimes they are shifted toward the blue end. That means the light source is moving toward the earth.

How much have the lines shifted? By answering that, astronomers can work out the speed of the light source.

The shift of lines is called the Doppler effect.

Stars On a very clear night you can see between 2,000 and 3,000 stars in the sky. A telescope will show you many more stars. But even then you have seen only a handful of the stars in the universe. There are billions and billions and billions of stars.

The stars you see at night are twinkling points of light. They look tiny, but that is because they are very far away. A star is a huge ball of hot, bright gases.

Only one star is near us. It is the very special star we call the sun. By day the sun's bright light fills our sky and hides the other stars. That is why the stars seem to come out at night. They are present all the time. But we see them only when the sun's light fades.

The constellation Orion as seen with the unaided eye.

as seen with a small telescope.

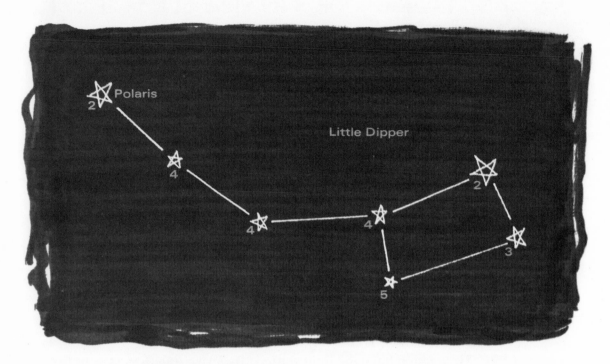

Polaris

Little Dipper

2

4

4

2

4

3

5

Stars of the Little Dipper with their apparent magnitudes.

The sun is 93 million miles away from us. The other stars are much farther away. The second nearest star is 300,000 times as far away as the sun. The stars are so far away that their distances are not measured in miles. Instead, astronomers often use light-years as a unit of distance. A light-year is the distance that light travels in a year. It equals nearly 6 trillion miles. The nearest star (after the sun) is Alpha Centauri. It is a little more than 4 light-years away from us. That is about 24 trillion miles. The very bright star Sirius is 8.7 light-years away. Other stars are hundreds, thousands, and millions of light-years away.

BRIGHTNESS OF STARS

When you look at the stars, you see that some look brighter than others. The ancient Greeks also saw this. They decided that the brightest stars must be the biggest. And so they worked out a scale of magnitude—*magnitude* means "size." They said that the brightest stars were of the first magnitude. The next brightest were of the second magnitude, and so on. The faintest stars were of the sixth magnitude.

Today's astronomers still use such a scale. But it is longer. It starts with negative numbers. The sun is the brightest star we see. It has a magnitude of −27. The second brightest star is Sirius. It has a magnitude of −1.4. The scale goes from negative numbers

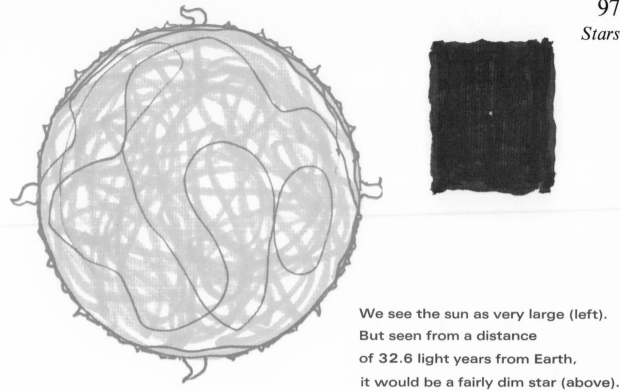

We see the sun as very large (left).
But seen from a distance
of 32.6 light years from Earth,
it would be a fairly dim star (above).

to zero to positive numbers. The faintest stars we can see without a telescope have a magnitude of +6. They are of the sixth magnitude. (Still fainter stars have magnitudes of +7, +8, and so on.)

This scale of magnitude tells how bright a star appears to be. That is, it is a scale of apparent magnitude.

But a star's true brightness may be very different from what we see. Brightness depends only partly on size. It also depends on distance. Therefore, astronomers also use a second scale. It tells how bright a star really is. It is called a scale of absolute magnitude.

For example, Sirius appears brighter than Pollux. But it is closer to earth. Suppose both were the same distance away. Then Pollux would shine brighter. Its absolute magnitude is greater.

To work out absolute magnitude, astronomers imagine that all the stars are the same distance from the earth. The distance is about 32.6 light-years. Absolute magnitude tells how bright a star would be at that distance.

The sun is very close to us. So it looks very bright. Its apparent magnitude is −27. But its absolute magnitude is +5. The sun is not really a very bright star.

sun •

Betelgeuse

SIZE, TEMPERATURE, AND COLOR

The brightest stars are thousands of times brighter than the sun. These very bright stars are much bigger than the sun. They

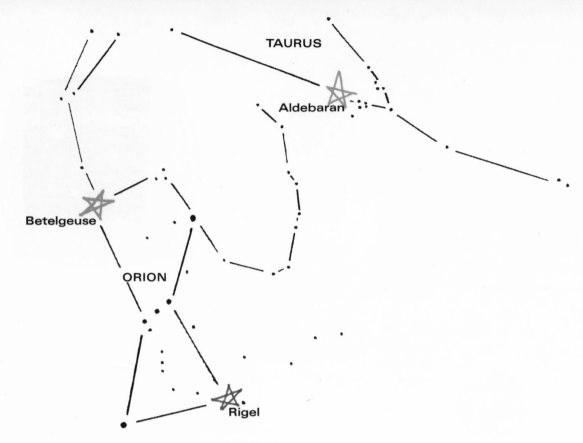

hottest star

coolest star

are usually very hot as well. Their surface temperature may be between 36,000 and 55,000 degrees Fahrenheit.

The dimmest stars are thousands of times dimmer than the sun. They are usually small and fairly cool. The surface temperature of a dim star may be about 5,500 degrees.

Astronomers can see that stars are different colors. The color depends on how hot the star is. The hottest stars are blue. Slightly cooler stars are blue-white. Still cooler stars are yellowish—the sun is one of these. The coolest stars are deep orange or red.

There are some stars, however, that do not fit into this pattern. They are the giants and the dwarfs.

Giants and supergiants are very big and very bright. Yet many of them are cool, reddish stars. Aldebaran, in Taurus, is a red giant. Betelgeuse, in Orion, is a red supergiant. But giants and supergiants can also be blue or blue-white. Rigel, in Orion, is a blue-white supergiant.

Some dwarf stars are hot and white, but they are also small and dim. (Most hot, white stars are big and bright.) These stars are called white dwarfs. Certain other dwarf stars are yellow, orange, or red.

DOUBLE STARS

Very often what looks like one star turns out to be two stars. The two stars are orbiting each other. Such stars are called double stars, or binaries. About half of all known stars are binaries.

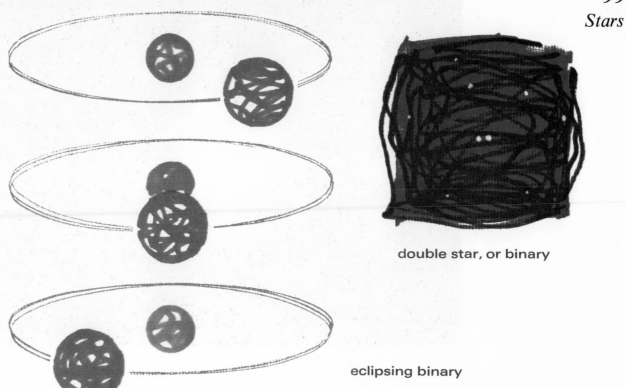

double star, or binary

eclipsing binary

Sometimes the two stars are much alike. Other times they are very different. Sirius, for example, is a binary made up of two stars that are very different. One is a big, blue-white star. The other is a white dwarf.

Some binaries change in brightness. They brighten and dim, brighten and dim. This happens because one of the stars is eclipsing the other. As seen from the earth, one star passes in front of the other and blocks its light. Such double stars are called eclipsing binaries. Algol, in Perseus, is a famous eclipsing binary. It dims for about seven hours once every three days. You can see the change without a telescope.

Some stars are made up of several binaries. These are called multiple stars. Castor, in Gemini, is a multiple star. It is made up of three binaries—a total of six stars.

VARIABLE STARS

Some single stars also change in brightness. Because their brightness varies, they are called variable stars.

Many red giants and supergiants are variable stars. Mira, in Cetus, is a red supergiant that brightens and dims slowly. It takes a little less than a year to brighten and dim. Betelgeuse is a red supergiant that changes suddenly. It shines steadily for several years, then suddenly brightens.

Still other variables brighten and dim within a few days or weeks.

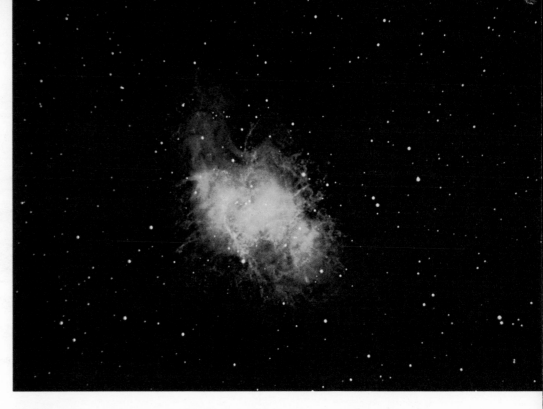

Remains of a supernova—the Crab nebula in Taurus.

A dim star explodes
and becomes a nova.

These stars are called Cepheid variables. They are named for a variable star in Cepheus. Polaris, the North Star, is a Cepheid variable.

The variable stars are changing in size. They grow larger, then smaller. That is what causes the change in brightness. But no one knows why the stars are changing in size.

NOVAE AND SUPERNOVAE

Every now and then a bright star suddenly appears in the sky. Earlier astronomers thought these were new stars. They called such stars *novae,* from a Latin word for "new." Today's astronomers know that novae are not really new stars. They are dim stars that have suddenly become very bright. When they become bright, they are seen for the first time.

A nova is a dim star that explodes. The explosion does not destroy the star. It is more like a giant sneeze. It blows an outer layer of gases into space. In about two days the nova becomes thousands of times brighter than it was. Then it slowly fades. Some stars become novae several times.

A few stars have exploded with much greater force than a nova. They have grown millions of times brighter than they were before. These stars are called supernovae. Supernovae occur very rarely.

Ancient Chinese astronomers recorded at least four supernovae. They saw one of these in the year 1054. Its remains can be seen today in the constellation Taurus. They are called the Crab nebula.

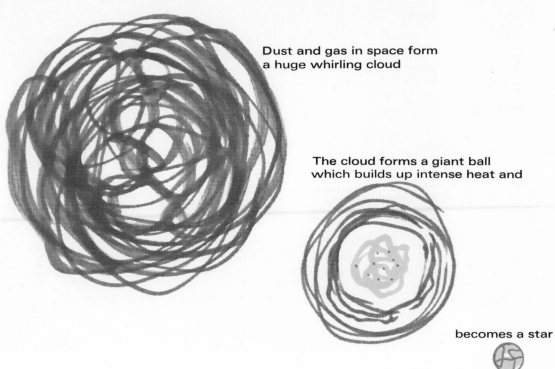

Dust and gas in space form a huge whirling cloud

The cloud forms a giant ball which builds up intense heat and

becomes a star

Astronomers last saw a supernova in our galaxy in 1604. But supernovae have been seen recently in other galaxies.

THE LIFE OF A STAR

Stars are born. They grow older, shining for millions or billions of years. And then they die.

A star is born out of a huge cloud of dust and gas in space. The particles of dust and gas whirl together. They form a giant ball. As they do so, pressure builds up inside the ball. When it becomes very strong, it raises the temperature of the gases. They begin to glow deep inside the ball. The glow brightens as the temperature goes on rising. Finally the outside of the ball begins to glow, too. A new star has been born.

The main gas in the star is hydrogen. Under great heat a change takes place in the atoms of hydrogen. Their nuclei, or center parts, join. As a result, atoms of another gas, helium, form. When hydrogen changes into helium, some matter changes into energy. It changes into heat, light, and other kinds of energy. This energy is given off by the star.

Stars use their own gases as fuel. When they use up all the fuel, they die. But a very small amount of matter can produce a very large amount of energy. Stars are big. They have a great deal of matter in them. They can shine for millions or billions of years before they run out of fuel.

See also: CONSTELLATIONS; GALAXIES; SUN; TWINKLING; UNIVERSE

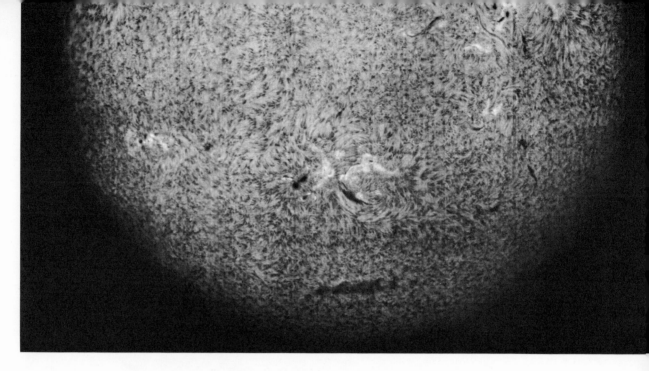

The grainy-looking surface of the sun.

Sun The sun is a star. It is a huge ball of very hot gases. It is so hot that it shines with its own light and gives off its own heat.

The sun is our star. It lights and warms the earth. Without its light and heat, there could be no life on earth.

Astronomers know far more about the sun than they do about any other star. The reason is the sun's closeness. The sun is about 93 million miles from the earth. The next nearest star is 25 million million (trillion) miles away.

As stars go, the sun is average in size. But to us it seems very big. Its diameter is about 864,000 miles. If it were hollow, more than a million planets the size of the earth would fit into it.

The sun rotates, or spins on its axis. The sun is made of gases, and so the parts of its surface do not move at the same speed. The part at the equator moves fastest. It takes about 25 days to turn once.

The sun produces a tremendous amount of heat and light. The earth receives only a tiny part of this heat and light—about one two-billionths. Yet this fraction is enough to light and warm the earth. The sun has been producing this energy for several billion years.

Where does the energy come from? What is the sun's fuel? The answer is that the sun is its own fuel.

The sun is made up mostly of a gas called hydrogen. Deep within the sun, atoms of hydrogen are under great pressure and heat. They keep turning into atoms of another gas, helium. As they do so, energy is given off. There is heat energy, light energy, and other kinds of energy.

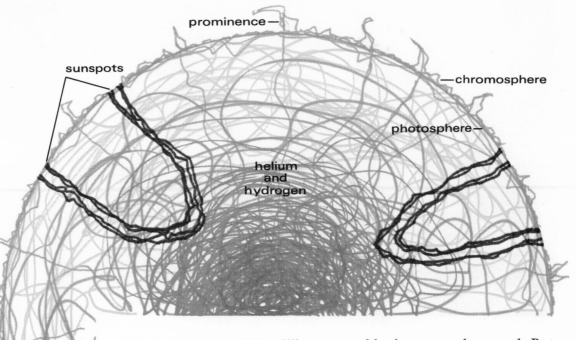

The sun uses up 600 million tons of hydrogen each second. But it contains a huge amount of matter. It has enough hydrogen to keep shining for at least 6 billion more years.

As energy is produced, it flows toward the surface of the sun. The journey is a long one that takes millions of years. When the energy reaches the surface of the sun, it escapes into space. The planets receive heat, light, and other kinds of energy from the sun.

The surface of the sun is called the photosphere. The name comes from two Greek words meaning "light" and "sphere." Most of the sun's light and heat are given off by the surface. The temperature at the surface of the sun is about 10,000 degrees.

The photosphere is a layer of gases. It is a shallow layer a few hundred miles deep. The gases in it rise and fall.

Photographs show that the surface has a grainy look. It is covered with dots, each a few hundred miles wide. The grains may be caused by fountains of hot gas. The gas rises to the surface in a jet and then loses some of its heat.

The surface is sometimes marked by dark spots 500 to 50,000 miles wide. These are called sunspots. Each appears to have a dark center that is surrounded by a lighter area. Sunspots, however, are not really dark. They only look dark because the surface of the sun is very bright. If you could see a sunspot by itself, it would be brighter than any man-made light.

All sunspots first appear as specks on the sun's surface. Then they may grow bigger. Big sunspots may last for weeks, or even months. Small sunspots vanish within a day or two. Spots often appear in pairs. There are years when many groups of sunspots

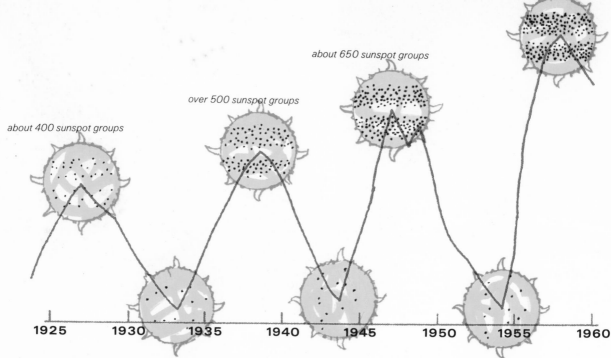

over 900 sunspot groups

about 650 sunspot groups

over 500 sunspot groups

about 400 sunspot groups

1925   1930   1935   1940   1945   1950   1955   1960

Number of sunspots reaches its peak every 10 to 11 years.

appear. There are other years when very few appear. Every 10 or 11 years the number reaches its highest peak.

No one knows for sure what causes sunspots. Astronomers think they are areas where hot gases have broken through the surface of the sun. Whirling and spreading, the gases cool. And so they shine less brightly.

Above the surface, or photosphere, there are still other gases. They form the sun's atmosphere. It is made up of layers. The layer closest to the surface is about 9,000 miles deep. It is called the *chromosphere,* which means "color sphere." It is a bright red-pink.

Clouds of different gases float in the sun's atmosphere. They look like bits of wool. They are usually seen above or near sunspots.

The sun's atmosphere is best seen during an eclipse. Then the brighter light of the surface is blacked out. Astronomers can photograph the atmosphere. (They never look directly at the sun, and neither should you.) They see what look like flames leaping up from the sun. The flames are called prominences. They are huge sheets of glowing gases. They reach into space for 30,000 to 250,000 miles. Usually the prominences leap up and then fall back into the sun. A prominence may last for days or even months.

Sometimes flares erupt above the sun's surface. A flare lasts only a few minutes, but it is very powerful. It is like an explosion. Astronomers see it as a burst of light in the chromosphere. Flares always occur on or between sunspots.

Prominence

Flare

Sunspots

The sun's corona, photographed during an eclipse.

The outer part of the sun's atmosphere is called the corona. *Corona* means "crown," and the corona looks like a crown around the sun. Gases in it form a filmy halo. The inner part of the corona is yellowish. It is about 300,000 miles deep. The outer part of the corona is white. It has long streamers that reach millions of miles into space. The corona is best seen during an eclipse of the sun.

Sunspots   *See* SUN

Supernovae   *See* STARS

Tektites   Tektites are strange, glassy stones. They are small in size and yellow-brown or greenish in color. They are streamlined in shape. They look something like drops of liquid that have frozen solid.

Nobody knows what tektites are or where they come from. But they probably have something to do with meteorites.

Tektites may have formed when large meteorites slammed into the earth. Rocks in the earth melted. Molten rock splashed high into the air. Drops of it cooled and hardened into glassy, streamlined stones.

Or tektites may have formed when meteorites crashed into the moon. Bits of rock were thrown off the moon. They were captured by the earth's gravity and pulled into the earth's atmosphere. There they heated up and melted. Later small drops of molten rock hardened into glassy stones.

Tektites have been found in several parts of the world. In the United States most tektites have been found in Texas. These are about 35 million years old.

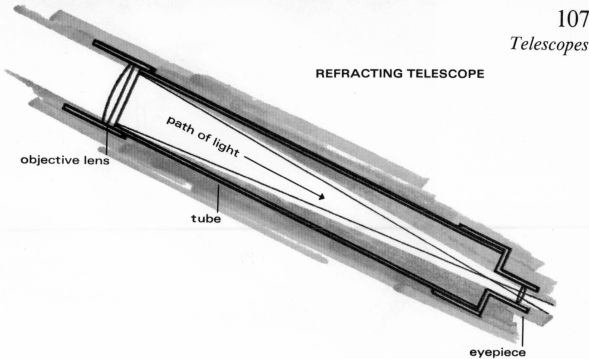

REFRACTING TELESCOPE

path of light

objective lens

tube

eyepiece

Telescopes

A telescope shows you many things that you cannot see with your eyes alone. You see features of the moon's face. You may see the rings of Saturn or some of Jupiter's moons. Stars appear bigger and brighter. And a telescope brings into view stars that you cannot see at all with the unaided eye.

The word *telescope* comes from two Greek words, meaning "far" and "see." A telescope is an instrument for looking at faraway objects. It makes them look nearer and clearer. This kind of telescope is called an optical telescope. The word *optical* means "making use of light." (There is also an instrument called a radio telescope. It is not used for seeing. Instead, it receives radio waves given off by heavenly bodies.)

An optical telescope works by gathering light. It receives light rays from a heavenly body, or object. It brings the light rays together, forming an image of the object. Then it makes the image bigger.

There are two main types of optical telescope. Each gathers light in a different way.

One type is called a refracting telescope. It has a lens at the front end—the end that faces the sky. The lens is a piece of carefully ground glass. It is thick in the middle, and it thins out toward the edges. When light rays from an object pass through the lens, they are refracted. That is, they are bent. They are bent in such a way that they come together and form a small image of the object. The eyepiece of the telescope is a second lens. It spreads the light from the image. In this way it makes the image bigger. That bigger image is what you see.

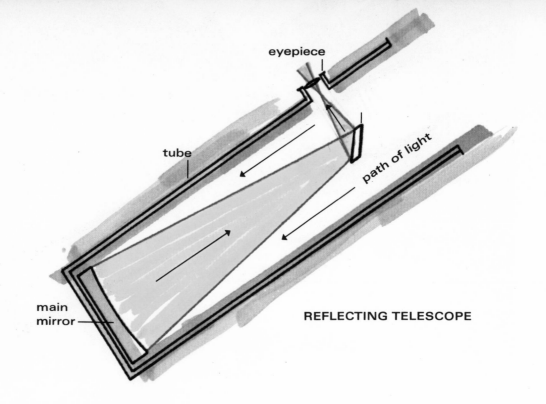

eyepiece

tube

path of light

main
mirror

REFLECTING TELESCOPE

The other main type is a reflecting telescope. It gathers light with a mirror. The mirror is saucer-shaped. The light gathered by the mirror forms an image. A lens in the eyepiece makes the image bigger.

Both telescopes show an upside-down image. In astronomy it doesn't matter if an image is upside down. You can study an upside-down Mars just as well as a right-side-up Mars. Correcting the image would mean putting another lens in the telescope.

The important thing about a telescope is its light-gathering power. This depends on the lens or mirror. A big lens or mirror gathers more light than a small one. It forms a brighter, stronger image. The eyepiece simply makes the image bigger. It cannot make the object seem brighter or clearer.

A refracting telescope is sturdier and easier to use than a reflector. It gives a little brighter image than a reflector of the same size. But the biggest telescopes are all reflectors. The reason is that they are easier and cheaper to make. It is very hard to make a big, good lens.

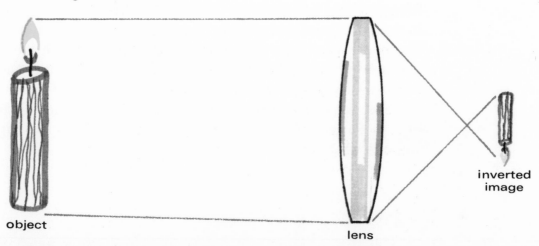

object

lens

inverted
image

200—inch reflecting telescope at Mount Palomar.

Light passes through the lens. This means that the lens must be made of the finest quality of glass. It must be carefully ground and polished on both sides. A lens is held in place around the edge. If it is big and thin, it will warp out of shape. If it is big and thick, it will not warp. But then it won't let all the light pass through.

A mirror is ground and polished on only one side. The light does not pass through a mirror. And so the mirror does not have to be made of perfect glass. A mirror is held in place from the back. It will not warp under its own weight.

The biggest telescope in the world is the reflecting telescope at Mount Palomar in California. The mirror in this telescope measures 200 inches across and weighs $14\frac{1}{2}$ tons. An even bigger reflecting telescope could be made. Scientists are talking of making a 400- or 600-inch one.

The biggest refracting telescope is at Yerkes Observatory in Wisconsin. Its lens measures 40 inches in diameter. It is probably the biggest lens that can be made.

See also: RADIO ASTRONOMY

Tides   If you have been to the seashore, you have watched the tides. When the tide is rising, the water creeps higher and higher on the beach. When the tide is falling, the water keeps drawing back. The rise is steady and the fall is steady. The level of the oceans is always changing. The name for their rising and falling is *tides*.

The tides are caused chiefly by the moon. They are caused by

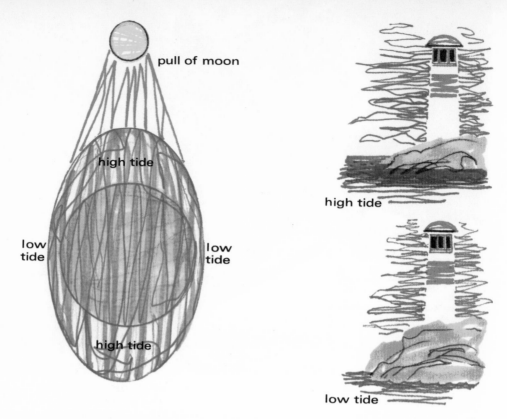

the moon's gravitational pull on different parts of the earth.

Imagine the earth as a solid ball covered with deep water. This is the easiest way to understand tides. Pretend there are no continents. There is simply one huge ocean covering the solid earth.

The moon is pulling on the earth. It pulls most strongly on the nearest part of the earth. It pulls the waters here into a bulge. The bulge is called a high tide.

The next strongest pull is on the solid earth. In effect, the solid earth is pulled away from the waters on the far side. As a result, a second bulge forms in them. It is also a high tide.

Between the two high tides there are two low tides. Water has flowed from them to the places where the high tides are.

WHY THE TIDES RISE AND FALL

Suppose the earth and the moon were not moving. Suppose they were standing still in space. There would be two high tides and two low tides. But they would always be in the same places. There would be no rise and fall of tides.

Or suppose the earth was spinning and the moon standing still. A place on earth would then have changing tides. The earth takes about 24 hours to spin once. In that time a place would have two high tides and two low tides. Each change of tide would take six hours. The next day the place would have the same tides. And it would have them at the same times.

What really happens is a little different. Every day a place has two high tides and two low tides. But they come a little later each

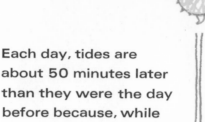

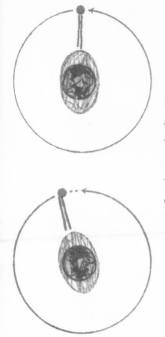

Each day, tides are about 50 minutes later than they were the day before because, while the earth is spinning once, the moon is moving ahead in its orbit.

As the sun's pull is added to the moon's, spring tides occur.

When it works against the moon's pull, there are neap tides.

spring tide

neap tide

day. The reason is that the moon is orbiting the earth. While the earth spins once, the moon is moving ahead in its orbit. A place on the earth takes about 24 hours, 50 minutes to "catch up" with the moon. Each day the tides are about 50 minutes later than they were the day before.

THE SUN AND THE TIDES

The sun also plays a part in tides. Sometimes the sun is in line with the moon and earth. Then its pull is added to the moon's. The earth has its highest high tides and its lowest low tides. These big tides are called spring tides because the waters seem to spring high. Spring tides come about once every two weeks.

Sometimes the sun's pull works against the moon's. Then there is not so much difference between high tide and low tide. High tides are lower than usual. Low tides are higher. These tides are called neap tides.

Time Your clock ticks and tells you the hour. The pages of your calendar tell you the day, the month, the year. With their help you keep track of time.

Our clocks and calendars take their time from two motions of the earth. Clocks are timed to the earth's spinning on its axis. Calendars are timed to the earth's journey around the sun.

These two motions make the sun and stars appear to move in the sky. Astronomers can measure the motions by using either the sun or the stars. The measurements give us two units of time: the

sunrise

noon ► **North pole** • ◄ **midnight**

sunset

candle
clock

Two early ways
of measuring time.

As the earth turns,
you are carried from
daylight into darkness
and back into daylight.

day and the year. All other units of time are based on these two.

DAYS AND HOURS

As the earth turns, you are carried from daylight into darkness and back into daylight. When your part of the earth is facing the sun, you have daylight. When your part is turned away from the sun, you have darkness.

Together the period of daylight and the period of darkness make one day. That is, one day is the time it takes the earth to spin once.

Long ago, people found a way of dividing the period of daylight. They had noticed something about shadows. Shadows are long in the early morning. They grow shorter as the sun rises. Then they grow longer as the sun sinks in the sky.

Men planted a stick in the ground. They carefully measured its changing shadow. They found that the shadow was shortest when the sun was highest in the sky.

They measured the time from the long shadow of sunrise to the shortest shadow. Then they measured the time from the shortest shadow to the long shadow of sunset. The two times were the same. That is, the shortest shadow marked the middle of the daylight period. It came at midday, or noon.

People then divided the daylight period into two parts. One was the part before noon. The other was the part after noon.

Later, people divided the two parts into smaller parts. And they began to divide up the period of darkness. Daylight was divided into 12 equal parts. Darkness was also divided into 12 equal parts.

Much later the 24 parts were named hours. The word *hour* comes from a Greek word for "time of day."

Today we divide an hour into smaller parts. Each hour is divided

sundial

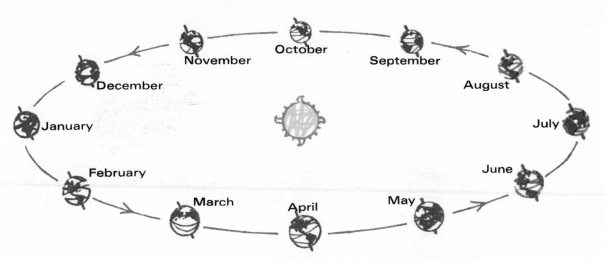

into 60 minutes. And each minute is divided into 60 seconds. Hours, minutes, and seconds· are all man-made units of time.

YEARS AND MONTHS

As the earth orbits the sun, the seasons change. They change from winter to spring to summer to autumn and back to winter. The changing seasons were probably the first calendar that people used. The four seasons gave them a length of time that we call a year. One year is the time it takes the earth to journey once around the sun.

While it is orbiting the sun, the earth is also spinning. During one orbit the earth spins about $365\frac{1}{4}$ times. To put it another way, there are about $365\frac{1}{4}$ days in a year. A fraction of a day is awkward. So we do not use it. In a calendar there are three years of 365 days. Then there is leap year—a year with 366 days. The extra day is made up from the four fractions.

The seasons were one early calendar. The phases of the moon were another. People saw that the face of the moon changed. It took about 30 days for the moon to go from full moon to full moon. This meant that people could measure time by the moon. They found that during the four seasons the moon went through its phases 12 times. That is how the year came to be divided into 12 months.

We still divide the year into 12 parts called months. But our months are not based on the moon's phases. The reason is that the moon goes through its phases every 29 or 30 days. Twelve moon months add up to 354 days, and that does not make a year. It is 11 days short. Our months are man-made units that fit the year.

We also divide the year into 52 weeks. The week is a man-made unit of time.

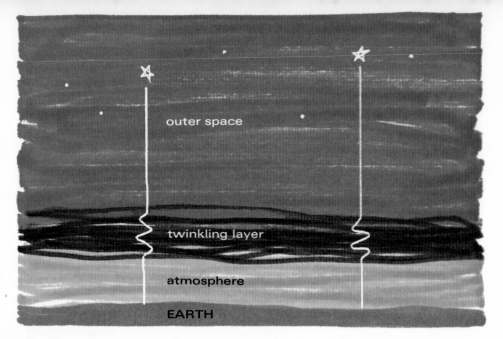

outer space

twinkling layer

atmosphere

EARTH

Twinkling   Watch a star and you will see that its light keeps changing. In the wink of an eye it brightens and dims, brightens and dims. This rapid change of brightness is called twinkling. It is caused by the earth's atmosphere and not by the star itself.

Light from the star passes into the atmosphere. About six miles above the earth's surface there is a layer of air called the twinkling layer. Here something happens to light from a star. It shifts and changes and seems unsteady. That is, the light twinkles. This twinkling light is what we see.

Astronomers are not sure of what happens to starlight in the twinkling layer. They think the layer is full of currents of moving air. Some currents are warmer than others. Some hold more water vapor. Light does not pass through such air in straight rays. With each change of air the rays are bent. That is probably why the stars appear to twinkle.

Universe   For many, many years learned men thought that the earth was the center of the universe. They thought that the sun and stars and planets all moved around the earth. About 400 years ago astronomers began to discover the truth. They discovered that the earth was not the center of the universe. It was a planet that moved around the sun.

Since then discovery has followed discovery. Today we know that the universe is huge beyond imagining. And seen against the universe, the earth is small beyond imagining.

The earth is one of a family of nine planets. The planets orbit a star, which we call the sun. The sun belongs to a huge "island" of stars. Such an island is called a galaxy.

Every star that you see in the sky belongs to the same galaxy. So does the band of light called the Milky Way. The Milky Way is

Earth is part of the solar system

which is part of a galaxy

which is part of the universe

which is made up of millions
of galaxies in space

The Andromeda galaxy can be seen without a telescope.

made up of countless, distant stars. Like the stars we see, it is part of our galaxy, which is called the Milky Way galaxy.

Our galaxy has about 100 billion stars. It also contains huge clouds of gas and dust. Still more gas and dust is spread out among the stars. The galaxy is 100,000 light-years long and 20,000 light-years thick in the middle. (One light-year equals nearly 6 trillion miles.)

But our galaxy alone does not make up the universe. There are millions of galaxies in space. There may be 100 million galaxies each with 100 billion stars. And then there are millions of smaller galaxies, called dwarf galaxies.

From the Northern Hemisphere only one of these other galaxies can be seen without a telescope. It appears as a hazy patch in the constellation Andromeda. It is about 2 million light-years away from us.

Some other hazy patches can also be seen in the sky. But they are not galaxies. They are huge clouds of gas and dust, called nebulae. If you have a good pair of field glasses, you can see a nebula in Orion. Find the bottom star in Orion's sword. Just above it you will see the cloudy patch that is a nebula.

Astronomers have also discovered some objects that they call quasars. Quasars look like stars. But they give off tremendous quantities of light and radio waves. They give off billions of times more than any star could. Quasars are the brightest objects in the universe. But they look dim because they are billions of light-years away from us. At present no one knows what quasars are.

Great gulfs of space separate the galaxies. One galaxy is usually hundreds of thousands of light-years away from its nearest neighbor. But the galaxies are not evenly spread through space. Some occur in groups. A group is made up of 10 or more large galaxies. It also contains some dwarfs. Other galaxies occur in clusters. A cluster is

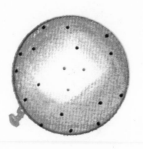

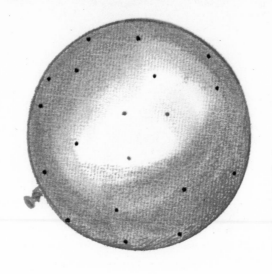

As the balloon expands, the dots move away from each other. Astronomers think the galaxies are rushing away from each other in the same way.

bigger than a group. It may have a thousand or more large galaxies and a great many dwarfs.

Our own galaxy is a member of what astronomers call the local group. The Andromeda galaxy is also part of this group.

One group or cluster may be 20 million light-years from the next. The most distant clusters known are billions of light-years away from the Milky Way. There may well be other galaxies beyond these. No one knows how big the universe is.

The galaxies are in motion. Each galaxy rotates, or turns around its center. And each galaxy is moving in space. A few seem to be moving toward us. Most are moving away.

They move at very great speeds. The galaxies that are fairly close to us move at about 700 miles a second. Distant galaxies are moving at a speed of 90,000 miles a second. That is about half the speed at which light travels. More distant galaxies may be moving even faster.

Astronomers think that the universe is expanding, or growing bigger. This seems the only way to explain the movements of galaxies in space. You could think of them as spots painted on the outside of a balloon. The balloon keeps growing bigger and bigger. And so the spots keep moving away from one another.

Billions of galaxies are rushing away from one another. This seems to be a fact. From it astronomers have built their ideas of how the universe began. Today there are two main ideas.

Some astronomers think that the universe began as a giant atom. The atom exploded. And from it came all the matter of which the universe is made. Gas and dust formed. Then galaxies formed out of the gas and dust. The force of the explosion sent the galaxies rushing outward. This idea is called the "big-bang" theory of the universe. Some big-bang astronomers think the galaxies will rush on forever. Others think that in time the galaxies will slow

"Steady-state" theory says that, as galaxies rush from the universe that can be seen, they are replaced by new galaxies.

down. Then they will stop and fall back together.

Still other astronomers think that new atoms are being made all the time in the universe. The atoms become gas and dust. The gas and dust become galaxies. Galaxies keep rushing out of the universe that can be seen. But new galaxies keep taking their place. Therefore the universe has always been the same. It will always be the same. There never was a time when it began. And it will never end. This idea is called the "steady-state" theory of the universe.

See also: GALAXIES; MILKY WAY; NEBULAE; QUASARS; STARS

Uranus

Uranus is the seventh planet out from the sun. It is the most distant planet that can be seen without a telescope. But it is small and faint in the sky. You must know exactly where to look for it.

Uranus looks small because it is very far away. Actually, it is one of the giant planets. Its diameter is more than $3\frac{1}{2}$ times that of the earth. Like its big neighbors, Uranus is wrapped in thick clouds. The tops of the clouds are all we see of the planet. A telescope shows that they are greenish in color. A more silvery band circles the planet at its equator. No one knows what lies beneath the clouds.

EARTH

URANUS

Uranus gets very little heat from the sun. But new research shows that its surface temperature is about −200 degrees Fahrenheit. This is about 100 degrees warmer than the sun's heat could make it. Perhaps something inside Uranus is warming the planet.

Being far from the sun, Uranus travels a big orbit. It takes 84 earth years to make one trip around the sun. It spins once every 10 hours, 45 minutes.

There is an odd thing about Uranus. Its axis is tilted much more than those of the other planets. The other planets are more or less upright in their orbits. Uranus seems to be lying on its side and spinning.

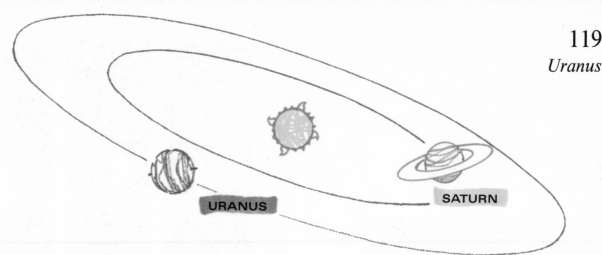

URANUS

SATURN

Uranus' axis is tilted so much that the planet seems to be lying on its side.

Astronomers were a long time learning that Uranus was a planet. Over the years the faint light of Uranus was seen about a hundred times. Each time the light was thought of as a star.

Then in 1781 Uranus was seen by the English astronomer William Herschel. Herschel had built a fine, new telescope. One night he was studying the constellation Gemini through it. He found a light that was not one of Gemini's stars. A star is a twinkling point of light. Herschel's telescope showed a glowing disk. He studied the disk night after night. And he saw that it was moving among the stars of Gemini. Herschel decided that he had discovered a comet.

Other astronomers eagerly began to study Herschel's comet. They began to plot its orbit. And they discovered that it was not a comet but a planet. It was a planet orbiting the sun beyond Saturn.

Uranus has five moons. Two of them were also discovered by Herschel. Small and dim, the moons are hard to study. The largest of them is Titania. It is about 1,000 miles in diameter. The smallest is about 200 miles in diameter. It was discovered only in 1948.

URANUS

average diameter	29,400 miles
average distance from sun	1,783,000,000 miles
average speed in orbit	15,310 miles an hour
time to orbit once	about 84 earth years
time to spin once	10 hours, 45 minutes
temperature at surface	−200° F.
moons known	5: Miranda, Ariel, Umbriel, Titania, Oberon.

Variable Stars   *See* STARS

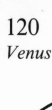

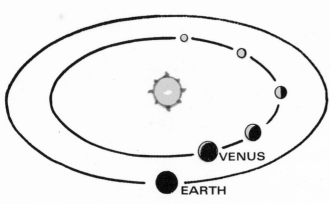

The phases of Venus, seen from the earth.

Venus In some ways Venus is much like the earth. It is an earth-sized planet. Its gravity holds an atmosphere about the size of our own. And Venus is in the same part of the solar system as the earth. It is the second planet out from the sun. The earth is the third.

Venus lies between the earth and the sun. That is why it never crosses our sky at night. Like Mercury, it appears just after sunset or just before sunrise. Even so, there are times when Venus is one of the brightest objects in our sky. It is so bright that you can see it by day.

Venus appears very bright for two reasons.

One is that it is our close neighbor. It is closer to us than any other planet. At times it comes within 26 million miles of the earth.

The other reason is that Venus is wrapped in thick, white clouds. The clouds reflect light well. And so Venus gleams in the sky.

The clouds make Venus a planet of mystery. Venus comes close to us. It is big and bright in our sky. But we cannot see its surface. The biggest telescopes show only the tops of the clouds. No one has ever seen the planet's surface.

Someday rockets will land on Venus. Their cameras and other instruments will tell us about the surface. Until then astronomers must study Venus in other ways. They study the clouds. And they are starting to reach through the clouds with radar.

Radar is an exciting new tool for astronomers. A radar set produces bursts of radio signals. When the signals hit a solid object, they bounce back. By studying the echoes, scientists can find out certain things about the object.

In the early 1960's radar was turned on Venus. The signals passed through the clouds. They hit the solid surface of the planet and bounced back. For the first time, scientists began to learn something about the surface. What they learned was surprising.

EARTH

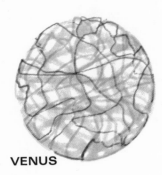

VENUS

 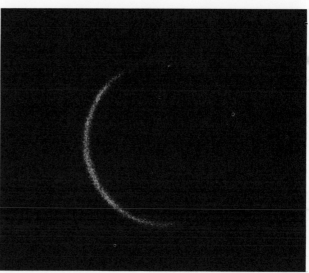

Radar shows that Venus rotates, or spins, backward—from east to west. On Venus the sun rises in the west and sets in the east.

Astronomers had long thought that Venus rotated slowly. Radar shows that it rotates very slowly indeed. Venus takes longer to spin once than it does to orbit the sun. It orbits the sun in 225 earth days. It takes 243 earth days to spin once.

Something else is even stranger. Venus always turns the same face toward the earth when it passes our planet. The earth's gravity seems to control Venus' spinning.

With radar, scientists are starting to map Venus. They have found two large rough areas on the planet. One runs 2,400 miles north and south. It is several hundred miles wide. The other runs east and west. It is even bigger. So far no one knows what the rough areas are. They may be chains of mountains. They may be fields of boulders. Radar does not tell how high they are.

Nor does radar tell how hot Venus is. To find out about that, scientists must use other means.

They have, for example, studied Venus' clouds. The clouds have large amounts of a gas called carbon dioxide. This means that Venus is probably very hot. Carbon dioxide acts like the glass in a greenhouse. It lets the sun's rays in. But it traps heat on a planet. It keeps the heat from escaping into space.

Other studies also seem to show that Venus is very hot. For example, Venus gives off radio waves. And radio waves are a clue to temperature. Radio waves from Venus were studied for three years. They showed a surface temperature of 585 degrees Fahrenheit.

In 1962 a United States rocket passed close to Venus. It sent back temperature readings of 800 degrees. But many scientists think that is not the temperature of Venus. They think the rocket measured the heat of a lightning flash.

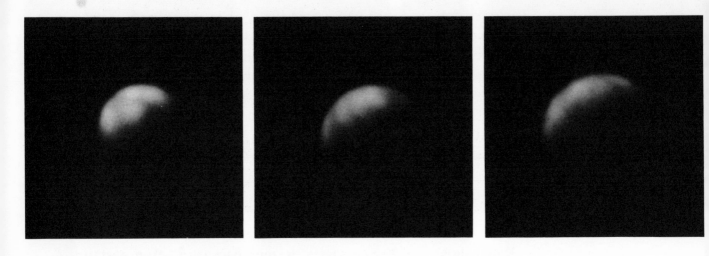

The shifting clouds of Venus, photographed over the period of about a month.

Almost everyone, however, thinks that Venus is very hot. Most likely the planet is a huge desert swept by sandstorms. It is dark, for the clouds are thick. It is dry, for it is too hot for rain to fall. And it is lifeless.

A few scientists do not agree with this picture. They think Venus is very hot at the equator. But they think it is much cooler in other areas. They also think there is water on Venus. The clouds of Venus contain water in the form of ice crystals. These scientists think that heavy snows fall near the poles of Venus. Melting snow and ice feed rivers. And the rivers feed oceans. They think that Venus is a very likely place to look for life.

See also: PHASES

VENUS	
average diameter	7,600 miles
average distance from sun	67,200,000 miles
average speed in orbit	79,000 miles an hour
time to make one orbit	225 earth days
time to spin once	243 earth days
temperature at surface	585° F.?
moons	none

Week *See* TIME

Weight *See* GRAVITY AND GRAVITATION

Year *See* TIME

Zodiac   The zodiac is made up of 12 constellations, or star groups. They seem to form a belt that circles the earth. Each month one of them appears in the east. Night after night it appears a little higher in the sky. After several months it has crossed the sky and disappeared in the west. Meanwhile other members of the zodiac are following the same path across the sky. By the end of a year all 12 have risen, marched across the sky, and set.

Ancient peoples noticed these constellations. They saw, too, that the moon always rose and set in the part of the sky that held the 12 constellations. So did the sun. And traveling among the same 12 constellations were five wandering lights. These were the planets we call Mercury, Venus, Mars, Jupiter, and Saturn.

This belt of sky seemed special to the ancients. So they gave it a special name. They called it the zodiac, which means "circle of living things." They chose this name because most of the 12 constellations were named after living things. We know these constellations as: Pisces, the Fish; Aquarius, the Water Carrier; Capricorn, the Goat; Sagittarius, the Archer; Scorpius, the Scorpion; Libra, the Scales; Virgo, the Virgin; Leo, the Lion; Cancer, the Crab; and Gemini, the Twins; Taurus, the Bull; Aries, the Ram.

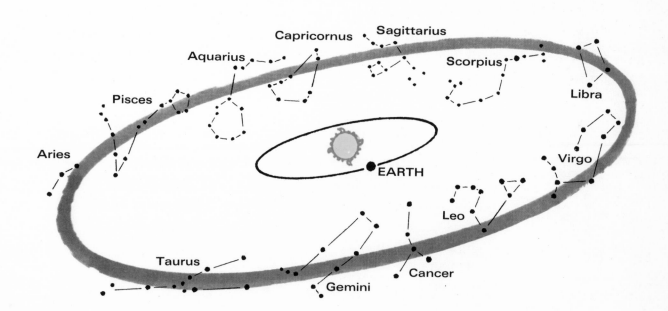